A Mirror for Americans

Related Publications by Cornelius N. Grove

Communication Across Cultures: A Report on Cross-Cultural Research. National Education Association, 1976.

Cross-Cultural and Other Problems Affecting the Education of Immigrant Portuguese Students in a Program of Transitional Bilingual Education: A Descriptive Case Study. Ed.D. dissertation, Teachers College, Columbia University, 1977.

The Culture of the Classroom in Portugal and the United States. *The Bridge*, 1978.

U.S. Schooling through Chinese Eyes. *Phi Delta Kappan*, Vol. 65 (7), 1984.

Secondary Education in the United States: An Overview for Educators from Abroad. Council on International Educational Exchange, 1990.

How People from Different Cultures *Expect* to Learn. GROVEWELL, 2003.

Understanding the Two Instructional Style Prototypes: Pathways to Success in Internationally Diverse Classrooms. *International Communication Competencies in Higher Education and Management*, Marshall Cavendish Academic (Singapore), 2006.

Encountering the Chinese: A Modern Country, An Ancient Culture, 3rd Ed. Intercultural Press, 2010 (1st Ed., 1999). With co-authors Hu Wenzhong & Zhuang Enping.

The Aptitude Myth: How an Ancient Belief Came to Undermine Children's Learning Today. Rowman & Littlefield, 2013.

Culturally Responsive Pedagogy. *Encyclopedia of Intercultural Competence*, Sage, 2015.

Pedagogy Across Cultures. *International Encyclopedia of Intercultural Communication.* Wiley-Blackwell, 2017.

The Drive to Learn: What the East Asian Experience Tells Us about Raising Students Who Excel. Rowman & Littlefield, 2017.

A Mirror for Americans

What the East Asian Experience Tells Us about Teaching Students Who Excel

Cornelius N. Grove

ROWMAN & LITTLEFIELD
Lanham • Boulder • New York • London

Published by Rowman & Littlefield
An imprint of The Rowman & Littlefield Publishing Group, Inc.
4501 Forbes Boulevard, Suite 200, Lanham, Maryland 20706
www.rowman.com

6 Tinworth Street, London SE11 5AL, United Kingdom

British Library Cataloguing in Publication Information Available

Library of Congress Cataloging-in-Publication Data

<to come>

∞ ™ The paper used in this publication meets the minimum requirements of American National Standard for Information Sciences—Permanence of Paper for Printed Library Materials, ANSI/NISO Z39.48-1992.

Reward children for good behavior? I think it's demeaning.

Japanese elementary school teacher[1]

Chinese and Japanese elementary school classrooms, contrary to common stereotypes, are characterized by frequent interchange between teacher and students, enthusiastic participation by the students, and the frequent use of problems that require novel and innovative solutions.

Veteran researchers Harold W. Stevenson and Shin-ying Lee[2]

Whether or not we envy other peoples one of their solutions, our attitude toward our own solutions must be greatly broadened and deepened by a consideration of the way in which other people have met the same problems.

Anthropologist Margaret Mead[3]

Contents

Acknowledgments   xiii

Preface   xv
    The Three Books   xvi
      The Aptitude Myth   xvi
      The Drive to Learn   xvi
      A Mirror for Americans   xvii
    How the Information in This Book Can Be Used   xvii
      Why East Asian Practices Can't Be a Model for Improving
        Our Teaching   xvii
      How East Asian Practices *Can* Be a Mirror "to See
        Ourselves as Others See Us"   xix
    My Reason for Writing These Three Books   xix
      Is Individualism the Solution? Could It Be the Problem?   xx
      Recognizing the *Values* that Drive Choices across East Asia   xxi

Available on This Book's Website   xxiii
    The Endnotes   xxiii
    The Annotated Bibliography   xxiii

Introduction   xxv
    Getting Reacquainted with Our Core Values   xxvi
      Concepts   xxvi
      Principles   xxvii
      Facts   xxviii
    More about the Research   xxix
      About the Time Frame   xxix
      About the International Comparative Tests   xxx
      About the Use of Generalizations   xxxi

About the Peoples of East Asia   xxxi
About the Apparent Tendency to Idealize   xxxiii
About Progressive Education   xxxiii
The Plan of This Book   xxxiv

1   Common Beliefs about Learning in East Asian Classrooms   1
The Stereotype of East Asian Classrooms   1
Example of a Mistaken "Fact"   2
    Why People in East Asia Aren't Concerned about Large
        Class Sizes   3
Two Reasonably Correct Facts   4
    Cram Schools Enable Students to Ace the Big Exam   4
    Learning Written Characters Gives Students a Competitive Edge 6
What We Know about Students in East Asia   7
    Four Research Findings   8
A Mirror for Americans   10

**2   East Asian Preschools, Part I: Where Children Learn
How to Live   13**
Vignette from a Day in a Japanese Preschool   13
    Teachers Ignore Many Childish Altercations   14
    Children Resolve Many of Their Own Disputes   16
    Children Have Lengthy Periods of Unrestricted Free Play   17
Japanese Preschools' "Pedagogy of Feeling"   19
    Two Types of Groups in Japanese Society   19
    Learning to Loathe Loneliness   20
Types of Japanese Preschools   21
A Mirror for Americans   23

**3   East Asian Preschools, Part II: Where Children Learn
How to Learn   25**
Kata as the Entry Point for Schooling   26
    Kata for Kindergarten Kids?   27
    "Entering through Form" for New Preschoolers   28
Kata as the Entry Point for Learning   29
    Learning to Share Responsibility for Effective Classroom
        Learning   30
Teachers' Relationships with Their Pupils   31
    Teachers Strive to "Touch the Children's Hearts"   31
    Teachers Mute Authority and Maintain a Low Profile   32
    Children Help to Shape Classroom Norms   33
    Children Rotate in the Class Leadership Role   33
    Periods of Reflection Evaluate Self and Group   34

A Glimpse at Chinese Preschools   35
A Mirror for Americans   36

4   Foundations of East Asian Schooling, Part I: How Children's
Learning Is Regarded   **39**
Thinking of Learning   39
   Virtue as a Component of Learning   40
   "Teach Books; Cultivate People"   41
An Excursion into the History of Ethics   42
   Ancient Greeks Valued Introspection   42
   Ancient Chinese Valued Extrospection   43
The Culture of Learning in East Asia   45
   Transmit Society's Accumulated Wisdom   45
   Instill Virtue, Conceived Primarily in Terms of Group Welfare   46
   Design Learning to Reflect the Subject's Logic, Not the
     Learners' Traits   46
   View Learning as a Challenging Mental Struggle   47
   Pursue Equity Goals, Not Equality of Opportunity Goals   48
A Mirror for Americans   48

5   Foundations of East Asian Schooling, Part II: How Classroom
Teaching Is Regarded   **51**
The East Asian Culture of Teaching   52
   The Analogy of the Composer and the Performer   52
   The Analogy of the Virtuoso Performer   53
   The Analogy of the Academic Expert   54
   The Analogy of the Pastor   55
   The Analogy of the Athletic Coach   56
Teachers' "Senior" Roles: Their Inclination   56
Teachers' "Senior" Roles: Their Opportunities   57
   Intensive Involvement with Pupils in the Classroom   58
   Extensive Involvement with Pupils Nonacademically   59
A Mirror for Americans   61

6   East Asian Primary Schools, Part I: How Classroom Lessons
Are Delivered   **65**
Setting the Stage for Whole-Class Learning   65
Teacher, Learners, Knowledge, and Interactivity   67
   The Role of the Teacher in Whole-Class Interactive Learning   67
   The Role of the Pupils in Whole-Class Interactive Learning   68
   The Role of "the Knowledge" in Whole-Class
     Interactive Learning   70
Detailed Accounts of Lessons in East Asia   71

Language Lessons for Chinese Third and Fifth Graders   71
A Social Studies Lesson for Japanese Fifth Graders   72
A Reading Lesson for Chinese Fourth Graders   73
Japanese and American Lesson Teaching Compared   74
A Mirror for Americans   75

**7   East Asian Primary Schools, Part II: How Mathematics
     Lessons Are Delivered**   **79**
A Detailed Account of a Math Lesson in Taiwan   80
General Features of East Asian Math Lessons   81
   The Stance of the Teacher vis-à-vis the Pupils   82
   The Handling of Pupils' Errors in Reasoning   82
   The Lesson's Pace and Degree of Focus   83
   The Nature of Classroom Verbal Interactions   84
Visiting Similar Lessons in Japan and the United States   85
   An American Lesson Introducing Fractions   85
   A Japanese Lesson Introducing Fractions   85
Specific Strategies of Math Teachers in East Asia   86
   Beginning with the Problem of the Day   86
   Emphasizing Abstract/Symbolic Reasoning   87
   Insuring Coherence; Making Connections   88
   Using Formal Proofs and Deductive Reasoning   89
How Teachers Build High-Level Thinking Skills   90
A Mirror for Americans   92

**8   East Asian Primary Schools, Part III: Other
     Performance-Related Topics**   **95**
More about The Knowledge   96
   Textbooks: Appearance and Use   96
   The Importance of The Basics   97
More about Classroom Process   98
   The Sequence of Learning Activities   98
   Asking Questions   99
   Patterns of Feedback and Discussion   101
Constructivism East and West   102
   Constructivism versus Instructivism   102
   Social Constructivism and Scaffolding   103
   Constructivism in the United States and East Asia   105
A Mirror for Americans   106

9   Knowledge-Centered Lessons   **109**
Labeling Classes Student- or Teacher-Centered   109
   Are U.S. or Japanese Classrooms More Teacher-Centered?   110

Are U.S. or Chinese Classrooms More Student-Centered? 111
The "Centeredness" of Classrooms versus Lessons 112
  Implications of a Teacher-Centered Lesson 113
  Implications of a Student-Centered Lesson 114
  Implications of a Knowledge-Centered Lesson 115
Lessons in East Asia: Knowledge-Centered 116
  Evidence for Knowledge-Centered Lessons in East Asia 117
A Mirror for Americans 120

Postscript **123**
  A Summary of What *The Knowledge Gap* Reveals 124
  Learning to Read and the "Reading Wars" 124
  What Does Science Say about Comprehension? 125

Bibliography 127

Acknowledgments

As in the case of both *The Aptitude Myth* and *The Drive to Learn*, my first "Thank you!" is for my longtime friend and professional colleague, Kay M. Jones, an eagle-eyed editor who also has the indispensable advantage of expertise in the languages and cultures of both Japan and China. Kay doesn't merely ensure that I write nothing I'll come to regret. She also keeps me abreast of matters such as the nuanced meanings of *tatemae* in Japanese, the accurate translation of an enigmatic quote from the *Analects* of Confucius, and even the correct spelling of authors' names. Thank you, Kay, for always treating my manuscripts as your very own!

For this project from start to finish, I've had five faithful "readers," friends, and colleagues who read my drafts and made suggestions for improvement. One has been with me through all three projects: Willa Zakin Hallowell, my business partner for thirty years. The others include Kathy Molloy, Walt Beadling, Laila Williamson, and Dr. John Gillespie. Whatever clarity this book has attained is due, in part, to their advice and counsel. For each of you: Thank you!

This book is based entirely on the published findings of dozens of anthropologists and other social scientists from around the world, each of whom devoted weeks and even months to field research in the preschools and primary schools of Japan, China, Taiwan, and Hong Kong. After years of reading, taking notes on, and annotating their numerous reports, I've come to deeply respect their thoughtfulness and commitment to accuracy. If I acknowledged them all by name here, I'd need include *at least* every author cited in my Annotated Bibliography on this book's website, www.amirrorforamericans.info. They all have my enduring gratitude for—and this is no exaggeration—making this book possible.

Preface

O wad some Pow'r the giftie gie us
To see oursels as others see us!
It wad frae mony a blunder free us . . .
Robert Burns, Scottish poet[1]

Oh, would some Power the gift to give us
To see ourselves as others see us!
It would from many a blunder free us . . .

This is the third of three books in which I explore the underlying reasons why American schoolchildren have been found, again and again, to learn more slowly, and to learn less, than schoolchildren in East Asia.

"Underlying reasons" refers to the quiet but insistent influence of *American cultural values*—the preferences and beliefs that most of us share regarding how people should conduct their day-to-day lives. American cultural values handicap our children from attaining the often-demonstrated learning prowess of children in East Asia. Yes, a few American children do meet and even exceed the standard set in East Asia. But considered as a group, American children lag behind their peers in East Asia academically and are too handicapped by our cultural values for most of them to catch up.

"Have been found again and again" refers to the results of international comparative tests that have been administered periodically to schoolchildren from many nations since the 1960s. The best-known tests are the PISA (Program for International Student Assessment), administered by the Organization for Economic Co-operation and Development, and the TIMSS (Trends in International Mathematics and Science Study), sponsored by the International Association for the Evaluation of Educational Achievement. Comparative tests aren't the only indicators of the relative academic attainment of students from different nations, but they are the measures most often discussed.

"Schoolchildren in East Asia" refers to children attending schools in Taiwan, Japan, South Korea, and China (including Hong Kong). Many hundreds of research studies focusing on children's learning have been completed in those regions over the past half century by scholars from around the world.

"Three books in which I explore" refers to *The Aptitude Myth* (2013), *The Drive to Learn* (2017), and this book, *A Mirror for Americans* (2020).

THE THREE BOOKS

The Aptitude Myth

Examined in *The Aptitude Myth: How an Ancient Belief Came to Undermine Children's Learning Today* are the historical reasons why most Americans assume that a child's inborn level of intelligence is largely responsible for how well he or she will perform academically. This assumption contrasts sharply with the one shared by most people in East Asia, which is that how well a child performs academically is almost entirely due to the child's own effort and persistence.

My quest to discover the deep origins of our myth of aptitude took me all the way back to Pythagoras, who lived around 600 BCE. But I found that the influence of Pythagoras and, surprisingly, of Jean-Jacques Rousseau and other well-known figures, was modest when compared with that of two others: Aristotle, who I hope needs no introduction, and Herbert Spencer, a British philosopher, author, and popular public speaker in the United States during the second half of the nineteenth century.

The Drive to Learn

I've long been convinced that the story behind American students' comparative academic weakness has two parts: (1) historical processes that led to our valuing a child's inborn aptitude over his effort, which I addressed in *The Aptitude Myth* and (2) a constellation of American cultural values that contribute in multiple ways to our children's relatively mediocre educational attainments.

When I began to do research for this second book, I thought of my mission as preparing to complement *The Aptitude Myth* by telling the second, cultural, part of the story in its entirety. That, in turn, necessitated addressing a range of cultural factors at work in children's homes as well as in their schools.

But as I worked my way through a mountain of published research, it became clear that there's ample reason to believe that what goes on in children's homes is at least as important, and probably more important, than what goes on in their classrooms. So the focus of my second book was the values and assumptions that shape the ways parents raise and socialize their children across East Asia and in the United States. It's entitled, *The Drive to Learn: What the East Asian Experience Tells Us about Raising Students Who Excel.*

A Mirror for Americans

What goes on in the schools of East Asia is very important, too, and has also been the subject of voluminous research. So the purpose of the book you're reading now is to explore that factor. In *A Mirror for Americans: What the East Asian Experience Tells Us about Teaching Students Who Excel*, you'll learn how teachers across East Asia deal with children during their most impressionable years, that is, while they're pupils in preschools and primary schools. Related in detail will be the values, concepts, and practices that are characteristic of classrooms in Japan, China, Taiwan, and Hong Kong. For a complete overview of this book, see the Introduction.

HOW THE INFORMATION IN THIS BOOK CAN BE USED

One might assume that my intention in writing this book is to hold up the values and practices of preschool and primary school teachers across East Asia as a model for improving American teachers' performance. Part of me wishes that could be true. But as a professional interculturalist for forty years, I know full well that comprehensive modeling across cultures will never occur.

Why East Asian Practices Can't Be a Model for Improving Our Teaching

The reasons why the teaching practices of one world region cannot serve as a whole-cloth model for improving the practices in another world region are bound up in the meaning of *culture*.

The culture of a nation or an ethnic group is not a cobbled-together collection of disparate ways of life. Over thousands of years, cultures develop into reasonably well-integrated wholes as the people within a geographical region gradually work out ways of handling the countless vicissitudes of survival within their ecological environment, and of relationships within their group and with nearby groups.

In other words, a culture doesn't originate as the result of a few people meeting together to thoughtfully decide what elements should be included. Each culture develops as the *unintended outcome* of everyone within a region, and across many generations, going through their daily lives in ways that increasingly prove reasonably satisfactory and predictable to themselves and to their neighbors.

A culture doesn't develop rationally or mechanistically. Rather, it develops spontaneously and organically.

Cultures are "reasonably well-integrated" but never perfectly integrated because it's inevitable that, among the myriad values, beliefs, and ways of life that make up a culture, a few will be incompatible. For example, one reason why cultures change is that some members become aware of a value-conflict and actively try to bring about change. In our own culture right now, we've become aware of a conflict between old, patriarchal ways of treating women and new sensibilities based on the American ideal that *all* individuals deserve equal dignity. Culture-change efforts such as this, and the backlash they inevitably provoke, get major media attention. Thus, many Americans become conscious of our culture's value-conflicts.

But what we almost never become conscious of are the ways in which our culture's values align and function very well. There's seldom major media discussion of our mutually supportive assumptions, values, beliefs, perspectives, and complex ways of successfully getting things done. Among the world's countless cultures, *reasonably* good alignment and smooth functioning is the rule, not the exception. So most cultures may be described as "reasonably well-integrated."

"Copy and Paste" Isn't Possible between Cultures. Because each culture is a reasonably well-integrated whole, it is not possible to cut a complex feature from one culture and paste it into another. I purposely said "complex feature" because in today's interconnected world people *do* adopt attractive features from distant cultures. For example, we have adopted others' foods (sushi), sports (ice hockey), and expressions ("ciao"); people abroad have adopted some of ours (such as blue jeans, basketball, and "OK"). But now we're not thinking about isolated elements of a culture. We're talking about the teaching of young children, which is one of any modern culture's most multifaceted features, steeped in historical traditions, shared values, professional research, governmental regulations, collegial sharing, and laypeople's expectations.

The difficulty of "copy and paste" is true in both directions, that is, not only from East Asia to us here in the West but also from the West to East Asia. During the late 1990s, two Chinese researchers studied the impact of Western progressive ideas on mathematics teaching in China and Hong

Kong. Here's their apt analogy: Education reforms based on Western ideas and implemented in Hong Kong are like *an organ transplant not completely accepted by the recipient's body.*[2]

Consider the practices of many Japanese preschools, to be discussed in chapters 2 and 3. Some Americans admire them greatly. But if Americans could copy some of those Japanese practices, then paste them whole-cloth into an American preschool, scarcely a day would pass before the school's principal would be placed under arrest.[3] The assumptions and values that undergird Japanese preschool practices are substantially different from those of Americans, including American values that have been codified into local and state civil and criminal statutes.

How East Asian Practices *Can* Be a Mirror "to See Ourselves as Others See Us"

Anthropologists of education and other scholars advise that, although it's *never* possible to copy one culture's complex educational feature and paste it directly into another culture, it *is* possible and useful to contemplate the values, principles, and practices of a distant culture as a "mirror."

Mirrors enable us, to some extent, "to see ourselves as others see us." By examining the assumptions and values that teachers in East Asia apply to a challenge that both they and we face—the teaching of young children—we might become able to see ourselves, as it were, from the outside. To the extent that we can, it will become easier to *consciously* recognize our own values and assumptions, reevaluate their effectiveness at guiding us to attain desired outcomes, and formulate fresh insights about more effective instructional practices *that fit well into our culture.*

Beginning with chapter 1, each chapter will end with a short section entitled "A Mirror for Americans." In it I will reflect on key facts discussed in that chapter, offering my perspective on the extent (if any) to which the instruction-related assumptions, values, and practices of East Asian peoples (a) help to explain why schoolchildren across East Asia learn more, faster, than their American peers and (b) help us to objectively understand the underlying drivers of the concepts and practices we use to guide and instruct the youngest Americans in our classrooms.

MY REASON FOR WRITING THESE THREE BOOKS

Many Americans, and especially parents, are actively concerned about the effectiveness of our schools. Even those who haven't heard of PISA and TIMSS know that all is not well. Our own ways of gauging students' learning, such as the tests reported at www.nationsreportcard.gov, tell an embarrassing tale about how poorly our schools are preparing children for adult life. And there are other, non-exam-based indicators as well, some of which are discussed in *The Drive to Learn*.[4] It's not surprising that there is, and there long has been, much discussion about how American schools can improve.

Among the themes of education reform efforts during recent decades have been free enterprise, child-centeredness, and accountability.

- Free enterprise counsels, "Let private entrepreneurs run schools with little or no government oversight."
- Child-centeredness urges us, "Find even more ways in which each child can become the focus of curriculum choices, lesson planning and delivery, and the teacher's attention."
- Accountability argues, "Distribute rewards and punishments to individual teachers based on how well their students learn."

All three of those educational reform themes are expressions of the tentpole American value of *individualism*.

Is Individualism the Solution? Could It Be the Problem?

Individualism is a way of organizing life on the basis of the beliefs that (a) each separate individual deserves more respect and attention than any group to which he or she belongs and (b) individuals are rightly the originators of ideas and the organizers and directors of activities, and each individual should benefit from his successes and suffer for his failures.

Because individualism is so treasured by a wide swath of Americans, big improvements can be promised by the advocates of ever more free enterprise, child-centeredness, and teacher accountability. Most Americans assume that individualism is the superior basis for planning and organizing work, play, and relationships, so they also assume that the application of ever more individualism is bound to improve outcomes for youngsters attending American schools.

These pitches for our typically American school reforms recall that amusing old definition of frustration: doing the same thing over and over again while expecting a different result.

Here's a question to ponder: What if our belief in, and commitment to, the value and ideal of individualism is not, after all, the panacea for American schools' substandard effectiveness?

And another: Could it be possible that individualism, *at least to the extremes to which we've routinely applied it*, is the main factor that has handicapped the effectiveness of our schools?

Recognizing the *Values* that Drive Choices across East Asia

This book will familiarize you with ways of schooling young children that are very deliberately *not* grounded in the values and ideals of individualism. Among cross-cultural specialists, the alternative to individualism usually is referred to as *collectivism*, *group orientation*, or *communitarianism*.

The greatest gain to be realized from learning about preschool and primary school teaching in East Asia lies not in the nitty-gritty details about "how they do it over there." After all, relatively little of what they do over there can be copied and pasted whole-cloth into our schools.

The greatest gain will come from recognizing that the assumptions and values driving the instructional choices of East Asian peoples are centered on the collective good of the students as a group, and of their families, their communities, and their societies.

That is the most useful insight that anyone can take away from reading both *The Drive to Learn* and *A Mirror for Americans*.

Cornelius N. Grove, Ed.D.
Brooklyn, New York
2020

Available on This Book's Website

Online at www.AMirrorForAmericans.info

At www.amirrorforamericans.info, you will find two resources that can extend and deepen your understanding of the text. Both are related to the research studies on which this book is based.

THE ENDNOTES

Any nonfiction book based on research, regardless of its topic, makes it possible for the reader to easily discover the specific research finding on which each claim in the text is based. This is the purpose of the notes, each one indicated by a small number within the text. Decades ago, the numbers referred to information at the bottom of the page and were called "footnotes." More recently, publishers began gathering all that information and placing it near the end of the book, where it's known as "endnotes." For *A Mirror for Americans*, Rowman & Littlefield and I decided to try something new: all of this book's 312 endnotes are at www.amirrorforamericans.info.

THE ANNOTATED BIBLIOGRAPHY

Any nonfiction book includes, on its final pages, a bibliography of the research publications—that is, the "sources"—that were consulted by the author during preparation of the text. *A Mirror for Americans* has a bibliography. But to simply list my sources seemed inadequate. The reason is the humane, qualitative nature of much of the research that forms the foundation for this book.

Familiarity with the anthropological research on which this book is based can aid your grasp of the ideas discussed herein. Anthropological research reports have a you-are-there quality that most other research reports lack because they result from an individual or team's entering a society to try to understand it *from an insider's perspective.* The researchers build relationships with local people and in some cases live among them for months as "participant-observers." Their reports include not merely their findings but also background details about the society and accounts of daily events that illustrate their findings. Anthropological research is quite engaging to read!

Therefore, available online is an *annotated* bibliography of the key sources for this book. Like the endnotes, my 118-item annotated bibliography is at www.amirrorforamericans.info.

Each entry begins with a "citation"—the author, date, title, and containing volume of the research report. Immediately following is my "annotation"— my overview or summary of that report. (None of the annotations is a copy of an article's "abstract," which is author-written.) The annotations are between 250 and 600 words in length, with most being nearer 600. Links to each entry are provided so that you'll never need to endlessly scroll down to find an annotation.

I have made these annotations available so that you may consult one or more to attain a better understanding of a section of the text about which you've become curious. I hope that, at least a couple of times while you're reading *A Mirror for Americans*, you'll pause to visit the online annotated bibliography in order to learn how the facts I'm referring to were gathered.

Introduction

Even the most elite U.S. suburban school districts often produce results
that are mediocre when compared with those of our international peers.

Jay P. Greene and Josh B. McGee[1]

This book is one of many that are intended to contribute to American school
reform. But it's one of few that, instead of urging readers to consider new
approaches to teaching, encourages them to reconsider the *values* that shape
their views about teaching.

Why proceed in this way? Because approaches to teaching are *choices* that
people make. What to teach and in what order; what materials to deploy and
how; whether and how to assess learning—these and others are choices from
among several options. Most books on school reform discuss choices; they
offer reasons why one choice should be preferred over others.

The underlying drivers of choices are *values*. Choices of all kinds (not just
in education) are derivatives of values. Values are foundational; they account
for the choices people make. In debates about school reform, when the various points of view are all informed by nearly identical values, transforma-
tional change will not occur. As noted in the Preface, many of our education
debates are about choices that revolve around the value of individualism. But
when all choices reference the same value, significantly improved outcomes
will remain elusive.

One way to become consciously aware of our own core values, and of
viable alternatives, is to look beyond our own environment to another world
region and ask, "Over there, what are the values that drive people's choices
about teaching?" That's what this book does.

GETTING REACQUAINTED WITH OUR CORE VALUES

The region known as East Asia is this book's focus because it's widely agreed that schools there are more effective than ours in enabling young-sters to master academic subjects. Two underlying factors account for their superiority:

- Their methods and materials differ from ours, a fact that's explained by the second factor:
- Whenever people in East Asia think about educating children, their thoughts are guided by assumptions and values that differ from ours.

As stated in the Preface, we can use the experience of people in Japan, China, Taiwan, and Hong Kong in delivering preschool and primary school education as a mirror "to see ourselves as others see us." If we can see ourselves from their outside perspective, we can *consciously* reacquaint our-selves with our own values and assumptions, reevaluate their effectiveness, and even be inspired to come up with fresh insights about more effective approaches.

In fashioning a mirror in which we can see ourselves as others see us, this book will make use of selected *concepts*, *principles*, and *facts*.

Concepts

The concepts applied in this book come largely from the professional fields of education and intercultural communication. It's likely that education needs no explanation. But some readers might not be well acquainted with the field of intercultural communication.

Founded over sixty years ago, intercultural communication is a research-driven, scholarly field that's closely related to anthropology and ethnography. Anthropologists study the internal workings of individual cultures in great depth and detail. Ethnographers compare and contrast fea-tures of different cultures. Interculturalists pursue practical concerns such as ways of improving the working relationship among people from differ-ent cultures who come together for any purpose: to do business, to build a bridge, to unite in marriage, to teach and learn in school, and countless other purposes.

During my graduate studies at Columbia University, my focus was on the challenges that arise when teenagers from Culture A attend school in Culture B. My doctoral project investigated the cross-cultural dissonance that occurred when immigrant Portuguese students attended schools in a

Massachusetts town.[2] Subsequently, my focus shifted to exploring the cross-cultural differences in how children are both educated in school and raised at home. An opportunity to live and teach at a university in China during 1986 sharpened my interest in contrasts among the cultures of East Asia and the United States.

Throughout this book, several of the concepts familiar to professional interculturalists will play an active role in illuminating the cultural values that are applied in educational contexts here and across a variety of locations in East Asia.

Principles

The principles applied in this book are those of the social scientist, the researcher, and the scholar. These professionals notice social issues that aren't fully understood, and then strive to understand them by patiently investigating a wide range of related factors. If they're doing their jobs according to the highest standards, they consciously try to prevent their own biases and values from coloring how they gather and interpret their data, and what they eventually conclude.

In the Preface I disclosed that I've long doubted that applying more and more individualism—for example, free enterprise, child-centeredness, and teacher accountability—will cure American education. One might wonder, then, whether my interest in the educational practices of East Asian peoples has occurred because their classroom approaches are *not* individualistic.

I don't think so. For example, one way in which American educators try to apply more individualism is by advocating use of "constructivist" teaching methods in which learners actively construct their new knowledge.[3] So you might imagine that I would doubt the effectiveness of constructivist methods and be eager to discover that direct instruction in East Asia accounts for their students' superiority.

Instead, I was conscious of my skepticism about individualistic values in education. I tried to keep that view and other biases from influencing my work. Having maintained an open mind with, I believe, reasonable success, I found that primary school classroom research in East Asia reveals that teachers there (1) infrequently use direct instruction, (2) often use constructivist approaches, (3) think of constructivism differently from teachers in the United States, and (4) use their constructivist approaches *very* effectively! (Constructivism is discussed in chapter 8.)

A personal goal that I've held in high regard as I've prepared this book is this: I will keep any prior views at bay and be guided only by research-generated *facts* about schooling across East Asia.

Facts

This book is based entirely on facts that have been (1) revealed by the investigations of hundreds of university-based researchers[4] and (2) published in peer-reviewed scholarly journals as well as in books from established publishers. This book's massive set of endnotes bears witness to my steadfast commitment to research-generated facts.

The researchers themselves mostly have been anthropologists who specialize in education, plus other social scientists who apply methods similar to those used by anthropologists. They hail from the United States and other Western nations (especially Australia), from a variety of other nations and—increasingly since around 2000—from universities and research institutes based in East Asia.

About fifty years ago, a handful of Hong Kong-based Western scholars realized that the new international comparative tests were revealing something no one had foreseen: Chinese students were attaining much higher scores than American students . . . *on every test!* This was unexpected because Chinese students were attending (what Westerners considered to be) dilapidated schools and being taught in "traditional" ways by "authoritarian" teachers, while American students were attending well-equipped schools and being taught using "progressive" methods by "child-centered" teachers. This discrepancy was termed "the paradox of the Chinese learner," soon renamed "the paradox of the *Asian* learner."

If you're a social scientist faced with a paradox, what comes to your mind? Research! So around 1970, the research began.

Fast-forward fifty years. I estimate that there are now well over 1,000 published research reports[5] that directly or indirectly explore every aspect of both child-rearing and schooling in East Asia. The raw material for my 2017 book, *The Drive to Learn*, came from 100 of the published research reports about child-rearing across East Asia. The raw material for *A Mirror for Americans* comes from 118 of the published research reports about schools and classrooms in Japan, China, Taiwan, and Hong Kong.

What this book does *not* do is tell you all about the researchers, their hypotheses, their methods, their subjects, and their data. Most readers are not interested in the processes and raw data of research, but only in its findings. So with almost no exceptions, this book will say nothing about names, dates, protocols, interview topics, sample sizes, and so on.

But a few of you *will* be interested in the nature of the research from which the descriptions and conclusions in this book are drawn. For you I've arranged an easy way to learn more about all that. In addition to the typical bibliography that's a standard feature of every nonfiction book, I've also prepared an *annotated* bibliography of the 118 research reports on which I've relied most heavily. You'll find my annotations, together with my endnotes, at the website created specifically as an accompaniment to this book, www. amirrorforamericans.info.

MORE ABOUT THE RESEARCH

The published research on which this book is based was carried out beginning in the early 1970s by anthropologists and others using mainly qualitative methods.[6] Their published reports cover a wide range of topics on differences between American and East Asian preschool and primary schools and classrooms. But the coverage is uneven. For example, you should be aware that

- Much of the voluminous research completed in Japan has focused on its primary schools and, especially, its preschools.
- Much of the research completed in China has focused on math teaching there, especially at the primary school level.[7]
- Findings from the relatively few studies carried out in Taiwan are generally accepted as reasonably congruent with the practices, values, and outcomes of schooling in China.
- Some studies have been carried out in Hong Kong (which until 1997 was a British territory), including inquiries into what happens when officials press Chinese teachers to begin applying Western methods.
- A substantial body of research has investigated what happens when circumstances put students from one culture into a classroom led by a teacher from another culture. Much of this research has focused on Western teachers of English leading classes of older students in China. In this book, this research area is referenced only once (in chapter 8).
- Few classroom research findings have been reported from South Korea. Therefore, Korea is mentioned only a couple of times in this book.

As in the case of *The Drive to Learn*, the information in this book isn't simply a condensation of the researchers' findings. Rather, I have tried to make their findings *understandable, easily remembered, and applicable.* My goal is to weave a story using plain English, providing readily understandable explanations, and summing things up concisely.

About the Time Frame

It is not the purpose of this book to compare primary schooling today in the United States and East Asia. If you're seeking information about schooling in present-day Japan, China, Taiwan, and/or Hong Kong, you will not find it within these pages.

The purpose of this book is to provide insight into factors that, *during recent decades*—roughly, 1980–2010—have enabled primary classroom teaching across East Asia to yield very effective learning outcomes for pupils.

In selecting research reports to rely on for my preparation, I have favored post-2000 publications over pre-2000 publications. But relying totally on post-2000 publications wouldn't be wise. A surge of East Asian school research occurred between 1985 and 2000, leading to the publication of hundreds of journal articles and books. Many are outstanding. They simply cannot be ignored.

Today, changes are underway across East Asia. For example, in response to the emerging knowledge economy, "Education for Quality" became Chinese government policy in 1999. Its goals were "fostering creativity and practical skills." Many specialists point out that China's new policy is marked by the fingerprints of Western liberal/progressive educators.[8] But this book is focused on *effective* schooling, not present-day schooling, so these changes won't often be mentioned.

About the International Comparative Tests

As noted in the Preface, the best-known tests are the PISA and the TIMSS. A third international test is the PIRLS (Progress in International Reading Literacy Study). A web search for any of these will provide you with more detailed information, including sample test questions, than you probably have time to wade through.

Each test is the outcome of thousands of hours of research, pilot-testing, and fine-tuning by experts in assessment, statistics, and other relevant specialties, drawn from many of the world's nations. Their efforts to improve the tests are ongoing. Among all those experts, one has entered public awareness: Andreas Schleicher, a German-born statistician who heads the PISA team. Information about Schleicher abounds on the internet, and he's often been interviewed.[9]

The most important fact about the international comparative tests is this: They do not gauge the quantity of academic knowledge that test-takers have amassed, so correct answers aren't the outcome of students' having memorized facts. What's tested are students' capacities to *apply* what they've learned to real-life situations. When author Amanda Ripley was allowed to take a PISA test, she found that on the math portion all of the formulas were provided, as was the value of pi (π). "But," she writes, "I had to really *think* about my answers. It seemed more like a test of life skills than of school skills."[10]

Keep in mind that international comparative tests aren't the only indicators of how well American students are learning academic subjects.[11] But of all the indicators, these tests are the most objective and the most often discussed.

About the Use of Generalizations

To understand the values, mindsets, and behavioral patterns of a *group* of people, we must think in generalizations. A generalization is a statement about a group's characteristic tendency or trend in thought, emotion, or behavior. It does *not* mean that every individual in the group is exactly like that. Nor does the fact that a few group members are not like that mean that the generalization is false.

Virtually every paragraph of this book contains a generalization. "Teachers in East Asia use constructivist methods." That's a generalization. It does not mean that *every* teacher regularly uses constructivist methods.

Everyone uses generalizations. We talk about occupations, age cohorts, neighborhoods, sports teams, political parties, corporations, extended families.... We rarely stop to consider each separate individual. If someone calls this to our attention, we'll typically agree that *not every* group member is like that.

Within each human group—family, age cohort, sports team—values and behavior vary. Culture is about *within-group tendencies and trends*. It's not about identical copies. The best way to talk about cultural patterns is to flexibly employ generalizations. Another way to talk about culture responsibly is to avoid, and to expose, stereotypes.[12] These are among the basic purposes of this book.

About the Peoples of East Asia

For the past several decades, the term "East Asia" has mostly been used to refer to China, Japan, Taiwan, and South Korea, plus the Chinese special administrative regions of Macau and Hong Kong. Each of these places has a unique culture. But most anthropologists agree that *the core values* of their separate cultures share similarities, especially regarding the raising and educating of children. In some research reports, these locations (often with the addition of Singapore) are lumped together and called "Confucian Heritage Cultures" (CHC). On many educational issues, research has revealed numerous similarities among these CHC cultures and a range of significant differences from U.S. culture.

Thus, in the following pages, Chinese and Japanese educational practices are often grouped together, notwithstanding the facts that their cultures have unique characteristics, and that these two nations occasionally have been on unfriendly terms, even to the point of armed conflict.

During recent centuries, the ups and downs of East and Southeast Asian economies have often been attributed to Confucianism. Economic expansion: credit Confucianism! Economic stagnation: blame Confucianism! While commentators oscillate between pro and con views of Confucianism's effects on national economies, one thing remains steady: acknowledgment of the powerful impact of Confucius's teachings on educational thinking and classroom practices across geographical East Asia.[13]

Confucianism is a set of principles for regulating and guiding individuals' interactions with others as well as the governance of public affairs. The foundation of Confucian principles is education or, more precisely, the value of the type of knowledge passed along from wise people, including not only publicly esteemed sages but also everyday scholars and teachers.

To the Confucian way of thinking, private life and public governance are both about human relationships and therefore about moral virtue. People learn the "how" of interpersonal relationships—that is, the "how" of moral virtue—as children. Virtue results from one's gaining knowledge—the kind of knowledge dispensed by formal education, which is organized learning from scholars and teachers. But the goal is neither to simply amass stocks of knowledge, nor to benefit from its practical uses. *Knowledge is worthwhile because it guides social conduct.*

For ordinary people to live together in harmony despite differences and inequalities, they need the virtue that education bestows. And for several centuries of Chinese history, in order for anyone to become worthy of joining the governing elite, they needed the highest level of virtue that education had to offer. Few restrictions were placed on who could attempt to rise into the ranks of the governing elite; the system was meritocratic. Success depended solely on who studied the hardest, as demonstrated by gaining a top mark on a grueling exam.

Principles like these provide a common undercurrent for the ways in which Chinese and Japanese people view children, learning, and teaching. Yes, there are differences in the details, but there are a multiple parallels in the broad sweep. Thanks to those parallels, preschool and primary school education in Japan and China may be discussed in a single document.

Nevertheless, this book will treat "East Asia" solely as a location on a map, not as the home of a single ethnic, racial, or cultural identity. And whenever the research warrants it, specific findings will be associated with Japan, China, Taiwan, or Hong Kong.

About the Apparent Tendency to Idealize

The generalizations in this book might give you the impression that the pre- and primary schools in East Asia are virtually problem-free. You could easily begin to think that almost every pupil behaves beautifully and learns prodigiously, and that the kind of dilemmas and frustrations with which we're familiar in the United States don't occur over there. That impression is likely to occur for two reasons:

- The purpose of this book is to illuminate the reasons why the academic achievement of students across East Asia has long been superior to that of American students, rather than to provide a comprehensive overview of education there.
- To remain *short and readable*, this book is focused narrowly on how pre-school and primary schools across East Asia work when they're working well.

Don't be misled: Educators in East Asia *do* face challenges. Not every child is a star pupil; not every class runs flawlessly. Some problems, such as bullying in Japan, resist solution.[14] It's just that in *this* book, we cannot afford to get sidetracked by such problems.[15]

And in any case, it's pointless to idealize schooling in East Asia. There's no way their educational approaches could be transferred whole-cloth to the United States; the basic assumptions and core values of American and East Asian cultures are too dissimilar. As stated in the Preface, we should be using the East Asian experience of schooling as a mirror that enables us "to see ourselves as others see us." Then we can reacquaint ourselves with our own core values and be inspired to formulate fresh insights about more effective ways of teaching that fit well within our culture.

About Progressive Education

This book mentions progressive education from time to time, so I'd like to offer a definition of it. For this, let's turn to our own American authority, Dr. Diane Ravitch, author of *EdSpeak: A Glossary of Educational Terms, Phrases, Buzzwords, and Jargon.*

> A philosophy of education that promotes active, experiential learning, as opposed to learning solely from books, lectures, recitation, and practice. Mostly, it is associated with child-centered education that is based on children's interests and concerns.[16]

THE PLAN OF THIS BOOK

In each chapter of this book, a feature of pre- and primary schooling in East Asia will be presented that, in my judgment, provides a piece of the explanation for why students there routinely demonstrate academic superiority to our students here. The book's larger objective, as stated previously, is to provide "a mirror for Americans" that enables us to gain insight into core values that drive our own educational thinking.

Chapter 1 reviews common American beliefs about schooling in East Asia. We begin here because many people "know" certain "facts" about schools in East Asia, facts that actually are false stereotypes. A few of those stereotypes are presented in chapter 1, as well as two other widely believed facts that are reasonably accurate. This chapter ends with a review of key findings about schoolchildren in East Asia that were revealed in *The Drive to Learn*.

Chapter 2 begins a two-chapter unit that explores preschools in East Asia. The focus of both chapters is preschools in Japan because far more preschool research has occurred in Japan than in any of the Chinese culture-based societies. This chapter reveals Japanese preschools as being where children *learn how to live* as members of Japanese society. Highlighted is the "pedagogy of feeling" that characterizes many of these institutions.

Chapter 3 presents Japanese preschools as being where children *learn how to learn*, that is, where they learn and practice ways of directly supporting teachers' efficient delivery of lessons. Also discussed at length is the nature of the teachers' relationship with their pupils. This chapter ends with a brief overview of preschools in China.

Chapter 4 begins another two-chapter unit that overviews the foundations of primary schooling across East Asia. In this chapter, the ways in which the peoples of East Asia think about learning are examined, in particular their assumptions regarding learning-related attitudes and behaviors and their value constellation that links learning with moral virtue.

Chapter 5 discloses a second foundation of primary schooling in East Asia, the ways in which classroom teaching is regarded. Surveyed are five analogies often applied to the teacher's role as well as their wide-ranging *non*academic involvement with their pupils. Teachers' long collaborations to improve lessons ("Lesson Study") are noted, too.

Chapter 6 begins a three-chapter unit revealing the characteristics of academic lessons and learning in the primary schools of East Asia, which is the principal focus of this book. This chapter is devoted to "whole-class interactive learning," the main lesson delivery mode, and to the roles played by the teacher, the pupils, and the knowledge to be learned. Four non-mathematics lessons are described in detail.

Chapter 7 narrows our focus to mathematics lessons, the most heavily researched of all lesson topics. Two lessons are discussed in detail, both of which are accessible on YouTube. General features of math teaching in East Asia are explored, as are specific strategies that teachers use to insure, via whole-class interactive learning, that their pupils make steady progress toward gaining high-level thinking skills.

Chapter 8 presents additional topics that complete the portrait of lessons and learning in the primary schools of East Asia. Included are East Asian textbooks (*very* different from ours), the key role of "The Basics" of any subject, various patterns of classroom processes, and contrasts in how educators in the United States and East Asia think of and apply constructivism.

Chapter 9 benefits from our new awareness of classroom practices in East Asia to step back and think knowingly about the meanings of *student-centered* and *teacher-centered*. Both terms reflect our own American concerns; they are not useful for describing lessons in East Asia. For that use, a new term is needed: *knowledge-centered*. That lessons are knowledge-centered in East Asia is a fundamental educational reason why students there always best their peers in the United States on measures of academic knowledge and its applications in daily life.

Chapter 1

Common Beliefs about Learning in East Asian Classrooms

Without data, you're just another person with an opinion.

Andreas Schleicher, chief designer of
the PISA international test[1]

Americans with an interest in the effectiveness of our nation's schools often pick up bits of information about schooling abroad. Gaining their attention since the 1990s have been schools in Finland, Singapore, China (especially Shanghai), and Japan. In most cases, though, what they pick up are isolated bits of data and, unfortunately, it's the shocking bits that they retain and share with their friends and colleagues. This is how inaccurate stereotypes come to be believed by the public.

In the case of Chinese and Japanese primary schools, there's a veritable mountain of accurate data drawn from hundreds of studies carried out by anthropologists and other social scientists. Let's use those research findings to evaluate a few of the common stereotypes.

THE STEREOTYPE OF EAST ASIAN CLASSROOMS

An oft-repeated stereotype of East Asian classrooms goes something like this: A teacher with a rather stern manner is lecturing to thirty to fifty students who passively listen and never ask questions. They rote memorize whatever they believe will be on the examination. Their prodigious capacity for memorization explains their high international test scores; actually, they understand little of what they've been taught.

1

This is a classic stereotype because, in terms of the "facts" it purports to state, it's not utterly false. For example, "Teachers always lecture." It's easy to find teachers in East Asia who appear to "lecture." However, they're concentrated in secondary schools, not the lower grades.

"Students never ask questions." It depends on what "ask questions" means. For most Americans, it means that a question is asked

- during class as soon as it occurs to a student (*when* it is asked),
- directly of the teacher (*who* is asked), and
- to clarify a point not understood (*why* it is asked).

If that, precisely, is what "ask questions" means then, true, students in East Asia never ask questions. But that *when-who-why* combination is highly restrictive; there are other ways in which questions can be asked and answered. Students in East Asia, living on the other side of the world in a culture unlike ours, *do* have questions and *do* get them answered—but they don't do it just like we do. (Question-asking will be discussed at length in chapter 8.)

"Students routinely rote memorize." To the casual observer, it would appear so. Actually, though, people in East Asia *agree* with us that rote memorization never leads to understanding. What the casual Western observer interprets as rote is something else.[2] That something is largely responsible for why many students in East Asia *do understand very well, and retain,* a great deal of what they've been taught.

Stereotypes about East Asian schooling are very difficult to modify because of their partial accuracy. They're largely based on the superficial impressions of casual observers who are unaware that their American values and expectations are, like glasses with dark lenses, coloring all that they are seeing. Once they make a value judgment—"Rote! How dreadful!"—they don't feel a need to probe behind the façade to discover what's really going on, as understood by the peoples of East Asia themselves.

Accurate understanding of East Asian schooling requires a *culturally contextualized* account of what "learning" means in that region of our planet and what, in practice, it involves. That's what this book is about.

EXAMPLE OF A MISTAKEN "FACT"

You might have heard it said that in East Asia, "class sizes are impossibly large." The claim that there are more students in East Asian classrooms than in American ones is accurate. The norm in Chinese primary schools is fifty to sixty, and "some classrooms are so crowded that there is barely walking space in the aisles."[3] But the claim that East Asian "class sizes are impossibly large" is a judgment based on American values.

Believe it or not, very large class size is not what teachers in East Asia worry about. And classes aren't that large simply because governments can't, or won't, hire more teachers or build larger schools. It's the way things are across East Asia, and people there are comfortable with it.

Here's a thought experiment: Imagine that you are designing an educational program in which a major goal will be to gently but firmly steer pupils toward becoming adults who will prioritize the needs and feelings of their group's members above their own. Among your many design decisions, you come to the one about class size. Will you make it easy for teachers to frequently interact one-on-one with each pupil, responding to his or her needs, feelings, style, and personality? Or will you make sustained one-on-one interactions with the teacher a practical impossibility?

People in East Asia believe that the outcomes for society are better if it's not possible for teachers to regularly pay individual attention to each pupil.

When an anthropologist showed Japanese preschool teachers a video of an American preschool teacher with a class of only eight youngsters, one of the Japanese women said, "I envy the way the American teacher plays with the children in such an uninhibited, 'barefoot' way." When the researcher asked if small classes are better, she replied:

> No, we didn't say better. Well, sure, better for the teacher, but it wouldn't be better for the children, would it? It seems to me that children need to have the experience of being in a large group in order to learn to relate to lots of children in lots of situations.[4]

Viewing the same videotape, Japanese parents similarly wondered if there wasn't "too little chance for children to enjoy spontaneous, unsupervised child-child interactions."[5] In Japan and China, attentive mothering is a good thing—when it's delivered by mothers. When it's delivered by teachers, even to preschoolers, it's smothering. Preschool signals that the time has come for something different.

Why People in East Asia Aren't Concerned about Large Class Sizes

Schooling both here and across East Asia has two basic objectives: social development and cognitive development. At the primary school level in East Asia, educators view social development as more important than cognitive development.

For example, in formal statements about the desirable outcomes of primary schooling in East Asia, social development is discussed at great length. A researcher who compared fourth grades in Tokyo and suburban New Jersey discovered that the "Lunch" portion of the Tokyo school's manual was *seven times longer* than the same portion of the New Jersey school's manual. Lunch in Japan is dealt with as a major opportunity to inculcate group-oriented social skills.[6]

Usually referred to as "moral development," social development is a constant, active concern of teachers in East Asia—in ways that you might find surprising. In Japan, there's even a textbook for this subject! (Children's social—"moral"—development will be discussed in chapters 2 and 4.)

Overwhelming evidence shows that in the early grades across East Asia, the development of children's group-centered, empathic attitudes and behavior is *a top priority for the schools*. People in East Asia believe that group-centeredness is best nurtured when classes are large.

TWO REASONABLY CORRECT FACTS

Anyone interested in East Asian education is likely to know about the so-called cram schools for exam preparation, and probably has marveled at the stupendous challenge of learning the thousands of characters that constitute written Chinese and Japanese. Some people wonder whether cram schools and character-learning give students in East Asia an academic edge over their American peers. Let's have a look.

Cram Schools Enable Students to Ace the Big Exam

East Asian "cram schools" number in the tens of thousands; some are big businesses. Scholars call them "mass tutorial schools." The Chinese call them *bŭxíbān*; the Japanese, *juku*; and the Koreans, *hagwan*. You might even have one in your neighborhood: Kumon. It expanded globally after becoming one of the most successful *juku* companies in Japan. Or maybe you try to solve KenKen math puzzles. Well, they were invented by a *juku* mathematics teacher for his students.[7]

For 1,000 years in China, a student's advancement from one academic level to the next higher level totally depended on exams, and ultimately on one, grueling, *three-day* exam.[8] If one's score on that three-day exam took him to the pinnacle of the academic heap, he was guaranteed to catapult into the top rung of society as well. So being meticulously prepared for the biggest of the Big Exams has deep cultural roots and engenders fierce motivation that's felt by students, parents, even grandparents and siblings. It's a family thing.

Given that stratospheric level of motivation, each aspiring family develops sustained interest in doing everything possible to ensure that their child aces any Big Exam and gets into the very best school. Here in the United States, a Big Exam—think SAT—is *one factor among many*; we also seek ways to leverage personal essays, recommendations, volunteering, extracurricular activities, personal interviews, advanced-placement courses, GPAs, and—for the very few—legacy and donor admissions.

But when a single Big Exam is literally *the only* factor, what leverage do families have? Their sole leverage is a child who has *thoroughly mastered* the material. Entrepreneurs in East Asia, seeing that need, have provided private schools that, for a fee, help students gain thorough mastery. Most of these schools are similar to those provided by American "SAT prep" firms such as Kaplan, Sylvan Learning, Khan Academy, and others.

Because cram schools are subject to little or no government regulation, they enjoy flexibility regarding matters such as class composition and size, subject matter, classroom methods, and teacher employment. Because they're founded on the profit motive, they must become and remain responsive to the perceived needs of students and parents, who are well known to be comparison shoppers. In the urban areas of Japan and China, dozens of these schools vie for the fee that most families are all too willing to pay, even if it means sacrificing other desires.[9]

Here's the thing: *the teachers must be respected and appreciated by their students*. The company's owners seriously need their teachers to be thought highly of; it's good for business. If a teacher draws complaints or is damned by faint praise: good-bye. Teachers who make a positive impression on their students, *and* whose students ace the Big Exam, can become not only wealthy but also, in some cases, local celebrities.[10]

Cram schools enable students to thoroughly master crucial subjects by giving them supplemental exercises to strengthen their memory and skills. Math speed tests are one example, but so is repeated practice in solving math word problems. The exercises, drills and, yes, memorizing that occur in these evening schools are a sound basis for rapid problem-solving and other practical applications that both extend and strengthen what the students learn in their daytime schools.[11]

But that's not all that goes on in these schools. Here's what one researcher wrote after her own inquiry into Japan's cram schools:

Juku create a homeroom-type atmosphere that youngsters find socially exciting, with the trading of notes, flirting, and the opportunity to meet students from other schools. *Juku* serve children as a neighborhood hangout spot more than one might expect.[12]

Some people in East Asia oppose cram schools because they believe that students study too much or that these alternative schools undermine the public system. Regardless of such objections, it's clear that as long as the winner-take-all examinations exist, cram schools will exist.[13]

Attending *juku*, *bŭxíbān*, or *hagwan* classes probably better enables students to ace the Big Exam that determines whether they'll be admitted to the top high schools and universities. Like SAT prep schools here in the United States, cram school teaching is focused on the Big Exam. One study in Taiwan was able to quantify the extent of students' learning gains as the result of each accumulated hour of cram school attendance![14]

Attending cram school classes very probably has no *direct* impact on students' performance on the international comparative tests. Furthermore, PISA, TIMSS, and other international tests have no effect whatsoever on the future of any student in East Asia or the United States. Students do not study for the international tests; cram schools do not prepare students to take them; and high schools and universities do not review international test scores as part of the admissions process.

Learning Written Characters Gives Students a Competitive Edge

If you're like me, you've looked at a passage written in Chinese or Japanese and marveled that anyone could actually learn thousands of characters well enough to read and write. Yet millions do learn them; languages that use written characters are among most widely learned of all languages. In Japan, children must learn not only Chinese characters but also two additional, extensive sets of phonetic symbols![15]

The challenge of learning to read and write characters far exceeds the challenge of learning to read and write using an alphabet. It's not only about the complexity of characters but also about the precision expected when a child writes them. Below we'll address these questions:

- How do adults in Chinese and Japanese societies teach characters to young children?
- Does learning to read and write characters bestow a general academic learning advantage?

How do adults in East Asia teach characters to children? Methodically and repetitively. Beginning in first grade (in some cases, preschool), the methods for teaching characters comprise demonstration, modeling, tracing, repeated copying, and active memorization of the placement, direction, and order of strokes. Invariably involved is the imitative production of teachers' models or textbook examples, which are to be followed with precision and endlessly practiced to the point where the child has them secured in mental and muscle memory.[16]

The traditional instructional sequence has been that a child learns to use a brush to manually shape characters properly before learning what those characters mean. Constant repetition is involved. The observable outcome needs to be, eventually, almost perfectly shaped and proportioned characters.

Keep in mind that character-writing is considered an art form as well as a means of communication. An art teacher who visited China to figure out how children there learn to draw so well was struck by the similarities between the teaching methods used there in both art classes and calligraphy instruction:

> First graders learn how to sit, how to hold the brush for the different kinds of strokes, how to prepare the ink, and how to mix the ink with water to achieve the right tone. In a fourth grade class, each child had a textbook containing rows of Chinese characters. Under each character was drawn the same character, but this time only with thin lines. Students filled out the lines in the lower characters so that the brush strokes were of the appropriate thickness and tone.[17]

Does character-learning bestow a general learning advantage? There are two ways in which this might be possible. The first is that learning characters might bring about physiological changes in the brains of youngsters in East Asia that would give them an advantage over their alphabet-learning peers. One quantitative study was able to demonstrate that, compared with Americans, Japanese subjects in six age groups (between sixteen and seventy-four years old) obtained significantly higher scores on two visual recall tests.[18]

The second general advantage that character-learning might bestow is this: the capacity for rigor, discipline, and perseverance that people are expected to acquire at a tender age might become a habit that is then applied to other scholastic efforts, such as mastering math. It is probably impossible for any type of quantitative research to empirically demonstrate this. Nevertheless, many scholars hold the opinion that the years of training in *learning how to learn characters* probably gives children across East Asia a competitive edge as they strive toward mastery of math and other academic subjects, an edge that could affect their international comparative test scores.

WHAT WE KNOW ABOUT STUDENTS IN EAST ASIA

The characteristics of the children who attend schools in East Asia are not explored in depth in this book. They are the subject of *The Drive to Learn*.

But that book isn't so much about children in East Asia as it is about how their parents raise, socialize, and infuse them with a passionate drive to learn—and not merely to learn in general terms, but specifically *to learn academic subjects from teachers in school classrooms.* As stated in the Preface of this book, there's ample reason to believe that the academic superiority of students in East Asia is explained at least as much by their upbringing at home as it is by the teaching they receive in schools.

For example, some researchers have compared the knowledge and learning skills of first graders in East Asia and the United States. Even at that early stage of formal learning, when the influence of children's homes is extensive while that of their classrooms is limited, young pupils across East Asia have been shown to be ahead of their peers in the United States.[19]

The main finding of my research for *The Drive to Learn* was that youngsters across East Asia arrive at the schoolhouse door "more receptive to school learning" than American children. But that's not because parents in East Asia have carrots and sticks up their sleeves that would work here, too, if only American parents would apply them.

Children in East Asia are more receptive to school learning *because of the cultures of East Asia,* which most children absorb from their parents beginning at birth. These are cultures that, for hundreds if not thousands of years, have been infused with almost reverent respect for academic mastery and— this is important—with high admiration for the effort that a learner of any age devotes to attaining academic mastery.

The outcome for the individual is this: If you happen to be born into a family whose values and behavior are sustainably influenced by one of the East Asian cultures (or another similar culture), then it's likely that you will develop into a school-age youngster who is relatively receptive to the kind of learning that occurs in school classrooms.

Four Research Findings

As noted in the Introduction, an estimated 1,000 published research reports have probed every corner of children's learning across East Asia. Nearly half of those reports are not about what goes on in children's schools; they're about what goes on in children's *homes.* They reveal the assumptions, values, beliefs, and practices of families in East Asia. From *The Drive to Learn,* here are four of the most important findings:

1. **Practical versus moral:** People in both the United States and across East Asia readily say that school learning is important. There the similarity ends. Here in our nation, we see the material to be learned in school

as important for practical reasons: to launch a high-earning career, to understand how the world works, and so forth. We know school learning is important—but for most of us, it's a cognitive conviction, not a deep emotional drive. In East Asia, the reasoned practical motive is accompanied by the individual's wanting to become a person viewed by self and others as virtuous and admirably moral. For many people there, that's a passionate drive.[20] In their cultures, one long-respected path to gaining a virtuous reputation ("face") is not only by mastering academic subjects but also by being seen to have devoted persevering effort to doing so.

2. **Aptitude versus effort:** Americans have inherited the belief that how well a child does academically is determined largely by his or her inborn intelligence. We're not blind to the usefulness of a child's own effort, but that's rarely our lead explanation. (My 2013 book, *The Aptitude Myth*, recounts how we came to inherit this belief.) Conversely, people in East Asia are not blind to the usefulness of a child's own inborn intelligence, but it's never their lead explanation for a child's academic progress or lack thereof. Instead, they point to the child's degree of sustained effort. For example, one researcher told of asking a Japanese teacher about her pupils' IQ scores. The teacher knew exactly where all the IQ records were kept, but she'd never bothered to look at them.[21]

   By the way, the aptitude/effort distinction resonates remarkably well with Stanford professor Carol Dweck's insights regarding "fixed mindsets" versus "growth mindsets."[22]

3. **Intrinsic versus extrinsic:** The distinction we routinely make between intrinsic and extrinsic motivation is useless in East Asia. Here's why: a family in East Asia usually is a close-knit, unified group. Members deeply share values, feelings, expectations, and goals; American-style individual uniqueness is definitely not encouraged. A family in East Asia is similar in some ways to a "superorganism," which in biology refers to a social unit of individual insects or animals that act in concert to produce an activity or outcome collectively intended by its members; well-known examples include bees and ants.[23]

   In the United States, the fact that Johnny's parents want him to study hard is, for Johnny, an "extrinsic" motivation, which according to Western psychologists is not an effective driver of behavior. In East Asia, what Reiko's parents want and what Reiko herself wants regarding her studying are likely to be identical or nearly so. It's the *family's* motivation and Reiko is a family member. Thus, Reiko's motivation to study hard is "intrinsic" even though it's also her parents' desire.

4. **Passive versus active parents:** American parents of a school-age child say they are very concerned about his or her academic progress. What steps are they taking to support their child's learning? The steps taken by many parents in East Asia make those of most parents in the United States look passive in comparison. The analogy drawn in *The Drive to Learn* (page 76) is that parents in the United States resemble cheerleaders, while parents in East Asia resemble athletic coaches and trainers. Parents in the United States tend to be warmly encouraging of good study habits and appreciative of good marks, always stoking their child's self-esteem. Parents in East Asia tend to coach their child's studying, pointing out errors and insisting that misunderstood material be revisited until mastered. (Self-esteem? That comes only *after* and *because* mastery is gained.) Parents are well known to purchase supplemental workbooks and to complete them side by side with their child. See the photo on the cover of *The Drive to Learn*, and then read the story of that photo's origin on the last page of the book.

A MIRROR FOR AMERICANS

As we Americans look into the mirror provided by East Asian preschool and primary education, what can we notice about *our* schools—and about the concepts and values *we* apply when thinking about schools?

- **Class size**: We probably didn't need the East Asian mirror to become conscious of the passionate drive behind our firm conviction that small classes are a "must" for superior learning to occur. What the East Asian experience reflects back to us is that our conviction is mistaken; learning outcomes superior to ours routinely occur in a world region where primary school classes of fifty or sixty pupils are common.

  The real reason for small class sizes is that they foster a school environment in which (Americans believe) children can be dealt with as separate individuals, each one able to have his or her own unique needs noticed and responded to by faculty members.

  The East Asian mirror reflects the fact that class size *by itself* has little or no effect on the quality or quantity of students' academic learning. Instead, beliefs about class size demonstrate differing cultural perspectives: a focus on the individual in the United States, and a focus on the group in East Asia.

- **Cram schools:** What the East Asian experience reflects back to us is that we, like they, make use of mass tutorial schools owned by profit-making companies. We don't refer to our version as "cram schools"; that's a pejorative reserved for *their* mass tutorial schools. Ours seem more dignified, perhaps because they're less linked—at least in our minds!—with that dreaded scourge of students: rote memorization.

There isn't much difference between our mass tutorial schools (mainly for SAT prep) and those in East Asia that focus on preparation for Big Exams. And remember that neither state-run schools nor private cram schools in the United States or East Asia prepare students specifically to gain a high score on any international comparative test.

- **Written character-learning:** There's nothing in our alphabet-using culture that comes close to demanding the perseverance and precision that children, beginning at an impressionable age, need to become literate in Chinese, Japanese, or other character-using languages.[24]

  Two researchers have noted Chinese students' consolidation of

  the linguistic skill to produce several thousand characters with deeply associated kinesthetic and aesthetic awareness and socio-cultural knowledge. Such practices are *likely to influence children's general ideas of learning* including repeated practice of models or examples.[25]

  In my opinion, *years of learning how to learn to read and write characters* is one of the factors that gives children across East Asia a competitive edge as they move on to study mathematics and other academic subjects, and that helps to account for their superior performances on the international comparative tests and other measures of the skills and knowledge that they study in school.

FURTHER READING

If you'd like more detail about the researchers' findings, or simply wish to know what inspired the contents of chapter 1, read the following entries in the annotated bibliography at www.amirrorforamericans.info.

- Biggs, John B. (1996), Learning, schooling, and socialization.
- Chen, Chuan-sheng, et al. (1996), Academic achievement and motivation in Chinese students.
- Jin, Lixuan, & Martin Cortazzi (1998), Dimensions of dialogue: Large classes in China.
- Jin, Lixuan, & Martin Cortazzi (2006), Changing practices in Chinese cultures of learning.

- Li, Jin (2012), *Cultural Foundations of Learning: East and West.*
- Rohlen, Thomas P., & Gerald K. LeTendre (1998), Conclusion: Themes in the Japanese culture of learning.
- Russell, Nancy Ukai (1997), Lessons from Japanese Cram Schools.
- Singleton, John (1991), *Gambaru*: A Japanese cultural theory of learning.
- Stevenson, Harold W., & James W. Stigler (1992), *The Learning Gap: Why Our Schools Are Failing . . .*
- Tobin, Joseph J., David Y. H. Wu, & Dana H. Davidson (1991), Forming groups.
- Tsuneyoshi, Ryoko (2001), *The Japanese Model of Schooling.*
- Winner, Ellen (1989), How can Chinese children draw so well?
- Wray, Harry (1999), *Japanese and American Education.*

Chapter 2

East Asian Preschools, Part I

Where Children Learn How to Live

> I want groups to become like families, where people live life daily
> thinking about one another.
>
> Japanese first-grade teacher[1]

There's no better place to begin than at the beginning: when a young child
shows up for the first time at the schoolhouse door.

This chapter and the next focus on Japanese preschools because far more
preschool research has occurred on Japan than on China, Taiwan, or Hong
Kong. At the end of chapter 3 is an overview of Chinese preschools.

Also, this chapter and the next focus on one type of Japanese preschool,
termed "relationship-oriented," which researchers have often studied. Two
other types are overviewed at the end of this chapter.

VIGNETTE FROM A DAY IN A JAPANESE PRESCHOOL

During the second extended period of free play, Nao tries to grab the teddy bear
away from Reiko. Reiko's twin, Seiko, intervenes, pulling on the back of Nao's
dress. The three girls fall to the floor into a pile of twisting bodies. From across
the room, teacher Morita-sensei calls out, "*Kora, kora, kora*" (hey, hey, hey!),
but she doesn't come over.

Eventually, Reiko emerges from the pile with the bear and then crawls under
the table, where it will be harder for Nao to get at her. Reiko tells Nao, "Stop it.
It's not yours." Nao says, "Give it to me." Seiko, Reiko, and a third pupil discuss
what to do. Reiko says to Seiko, "You should scold her!" Seiko admonishes Nao,
"That's bad! You can't just grab the bear away like that!" Nao responds, "But
I had it first." Seiko replies, "But then you put it down, so your turn was over."

Nao is led away by Reiko, who says, "You can't do that. Do you understand? Promise?" Linking little fingers, the two girls swing their arms back and forth as they sing, "Keep the promise or swallow a thousand needles." Reiko puts her arm around Nao's shoulders and says, "Understand? Good." Morita-sensei, who has been ignoring their altercation, announces that it's time to clean up for lunch. Reiko, her arm around Nao, rubs her back and leads her to the forming line of children.[2]

What would be the likely actions of an American preschool teacher who saw several girls fighting over a teddy bear? We'd expect her to rush toward them, pull them apart with a scolding, ask each girl to express to the others her own perspective, and draw principles for their future behavior. That *could* also happen in Japan because there are different types of preschools there (more about this at the end of this chapter). But Japanese teachers' hands-off approach in the face of misbehavior, even physical fights, has often been documented.

Three features of the above vignette stand out for many Americans:

- Except for calling out "Hey!," the teacher ignored the girls' altercation.
- Nao is admonished by, then taken under the wing of, her opponent.
- The vignette occurred during one of the children's lengthy periods of unrestricted free play.

Teachers Ignore Many Childish Altercations

Several research studies offer detailed accounts of pupils' misbehavior—or at least what we Americans would regard as misbehavior—and the deliberate *noninvolvement* of their teachers. In one of my favorites, a pupil runs up to her teacher during free play to report that Hiroki is throwing flashcards off the balcony. Her teacher coolly replies, "Is he? So what do you think can be done about that?"[3]

Morita-sensei, the teacher who called out "*kora, kora, kora*" while the three girls were struggling on the floor but took no other action, explained herself using the word *mimamoru*, which links terms for "to look" and "to guard, protect." She viewed her role as being alert for imminent danger but otherwise allowing developmental goals to be attained, not via adults' punishments and precepts but rather in the normal course of children's growth and maturation.

Japanese preschool teachers sometimes intervene, sometimes they don't. The key point is that they resist the temptation to automatically intervene and to preemptively protect. Instead, teachers balance the risk that the situation will seriously deteriorate against the benefit that pupils can gain from the natural social situation, which they themselves might figure out how to resolve—experiential learning at its best.[4]

The principal of a preschool said

> Perhaps one reason why we have big classes is precisely to assure that there will be fights. At home these days, children are supervised very closely by their mothers. Many have no siblings. They have little opportunity to play naturally with other children, in a childlike way, out of sight of adults. Children's fighting isn't the real problem. *If there were no fights, now that would be the problem.* We don't encourage children to fight, but if fights occur, well, that may be for the best, and the best thing we can do might be not to rush in and break them up.[5]

Problems from the perspective of Japanese preschool teachers: We've noted that Japanese preschool teachers do not consider fighting to be a problem. So what *do* they view as classroom problems? There are two:

- **Overreliance on the teacher:** New pupils have been dependent on their mothers. Now they must learn how to behave in society, for which self-reliance is a prerequisite. Preschool is where they learn this—and the learning can be rocky! Teachers are tireless in helping the little ones learn to do small things on their own while giving only minimal assistance. Teachers are capable of withstanding tantrums and waiting patiently. In fact, they're well known to have the *entire class* wait patiently while, for example, little Katsuaki, rebellious and sobbing, finally manages to don his traveling smock for the very first time (then to proclaim, "I can do buttons, too!"). By the way, that incident required nine minutes to play itself out.[6]

- **Nonparticipation in group activities:** Given the primacy of group-centered values guiding preschools, a child's willful nonparticipation always causes handwringing. Nonparticipation means either refusing to stop one activity and join classmates in transitioning to another, or—especially threatening—passive withdrawal. As noted above, having an entire class wait until a child is persuaded to join them is a typical tactic of teachers, who repeatedly remind the child that all his friends are waiting for him. Verbatim transcripts of these incidents reveal that the teachers don't appeal to rules, don't react punitively to a child's blows or kicks, don't invoke parental disappointment, and *never* say or imply that the child is a bad person. Instead, their strategy highlights the joys of peer togetherness.[7]

Problems from the perspective of American preschool teachers: The same question was asked of American teachers. One of their main concerns was *hitting*. American teachers think that hitters should be isolated. In Japan, the view is that hitters "don't yet understand" how to relate to others. Isolation won't help; what they need is *more* social contact.

The other American-perceived problem was *hyperactivity*. They are eager for their charges to develop self-control. Japanese people in general don't view the rowdy behavior of children as hyper-anything; boisterous enthusiasm is a desirable indication of character strength in young children (which explains why American visitors invariably describe Japanese preschools as impossibly noisy and chaotic). A researcher wrote that

> Japanese teachers regard even the most fidgety and hyperactive children with an affectionate amusement similar to what Americans feel for adventurous, gamboling puppies.[8]

Children Resolve Many of Their Own Disputes

We've seen that Japanese preschool teachers view their young charges' disputes not only as normal but also desirable—and not merely desirable in a "nice to have" way. Disputes are positively *important* to have, so important that teachers often count classroom materials such as art-table crayons and sandbox shovels to deliberately ensure that *there aren't enough to go around*.[9]

Three researchers witnessed—and videotaped—not only the quarrel over the teddy bear but also, the same day, a squabble over a sandbox shovel. They mentioned to the principal that fights might be avoided if more bears and shovels were available. The principal replied that

> if there are enough toys to go around, children do not need to communicate with each other. They can engage in solitary play, as they often do at home. But the purpose of preschool is to give children experiences they cannot have at home. It is through experiencing conflicts with peers that children develop social skills, individually and collectively.[10]

A teacher explained that by not quickly intervening in disputes, she gives

> children time and space to work issues out on their own. If teachers intervene too readily, children lose the chance to experience social complexity. Fights give children the opportunity to experience a range of emotions and to empathize. One day a girl might hit somebody, but on another day that girl might be hit. Children change their positions and come to know a range of feelings. People can't understand these feelings without having direct experience.[11]

American teachers undoubtedly agree that a goal for preschoolers is learning to share. They actively try to bring about sharing, often via precept and example. In Japan, the usefulness of sharing is more likely to be learned experientially. Educators there believe that, with relatively little adult input, many children will begin to realize the usefulness of sharing *if* they often are confronted with resource scarcity. And *if* there are enough fights, most children will figure out on their own how to resolve differences without fighting. The teddy bear incident ended with the antagonists walking off arm-in-arm. The squabble over the sandbox shovel was settled via a rock-paper-scissors contest.

Granted, not every dispute among Japanese preschoolers is resolved by the children themselves. Not every incidence of misbehavior is ignored by the teachers. But what multiple research findings are telling us is this: In broad comparison with U.S. preschools, Japanese preschools place far higher value on each child's experientially gaining a dynamic sense of community as well as a desire to build considerate, empathetic relations with that community's other members.

Children Have Lengthy Periods of Unrestricted Free Play

In many Japanese preschools, children spend half the day in free play. Free play means they're free to do *anything they choose* within the confines of the school property—with virtually no adult supervision. What, exactly, does "half the day" mean? One researcher calculated the average amount of time used on various activities by five-year-olds in the fifteen Japanese preschools that had hosted her:

50 percent in free play (see examples below),
14 percent in an art or craft activity,
8 percent in singing, dancing, or exercising to music,
7 percent in ceremonies, class meetings, or school assemblies,
7 percent in lunchtime or snack time,
5 percent in listening to stories,
5 percent in clean up,
1 percent in academic activities (e.g., recreating a pattern with blocks).[12]

Free play is an unregimented, largely unsupervised, exuberant, and very noisy time during which young children have the run of the school—classrooms, corridors, stairwells, gym, playground—for a total of approximately two hours a day. During that time they can be found

> donning skirts from the dress-up box; trying to hit the ceiling with balls made from crumpled colored cellophane; playing with water in dishpans inside the classroom; squirting hoses in the play yard; bringing large wooden blocks from

the gym to the classroom (these blocks are 3 to 5 feet long and very heavy, requiring children to carry them together); building playhouses in the classroom from the large blocks; playing with and feeding guinea pigs and rabbits; making an "irrigation project" with sand, water, and big plastic pipes in the sand area; making airplanes, dollhouses, robots, etc., out of empty boxes; playing on the trampoline, slide, swings, and other sports equipment; throwing hula hoops up the indoor staircase and trying to catch them as they come down; and carrying water and plastic dishes toward the stairwell to play house.[13]

When Japanese people think about preschool activities for children, their minds are applying assumptions, concepts, and values that contrast sharply with ours. Consider these:

- Small children do not need to be protected from every imaginable danger that *might* lurk in their social and physical environment.
- Children's spontaneity and high-spirited energy are age-appropriate and attractive; there's no sense in trying to contain or channel it.
- Children are innately good, that is, they never *intentionally* do bad things. Of course, they *do* need to learn their community's values and ways of life (which is the focus of this chapter).

The objective that can't be realized without lengthy free play: Driving many Japanese preschools is a determination to realize the preeminent objective that *these youngsters will gain an active sense of community*. Furthermore, it's important that the children do this not because of their teachers' precept or example, but experientially.

The children's naturally built community as well as their growing sense of group cohesion provide, in turn, the raw material that their teachers will use while gradually and patiently, yet persistently, aiming toward two crucial goals:

- to nurture the children's emotional bonds with one another, and
- to foster each child's development as a self-identified group member who feels empathetic and considerate toward fellow members.[14]

Japanese educators are keenly aware that, in their culture more than most others, expectations for how one behaves within one's home are unlike expectations for how one behaves out in society. We'll consider those distinctions later in this chapter. For now, suffice it to say that (a) teachers cannot build out-in-society behavior on the habits that children bring from home; (b) teachers do *not* see themselves as taking over the role of mothers; and (c) children must gradually come to recognize that their family-indulged habit of having things their way—*wagamama*—must now take a back seat to the desires and needs of their groups.[15]

But before such all-important objectives can begin to be realized, the children first must feel a spontaneously growing sense of group identification. It's the raw material with which their teachers work.

JAPANESE PRESCHOOLS' "PEDAGOGY OF FEELING"[16]

Japanese preschool teachers understand that their role is to teach children how to become social beings in Japanese society. They know that each child's strong ties with his or her mother are desirable, beneficial—and appropriate within the nuclear family. Teachers look for ways to develop within the children similar ties and the emotions they engender, orienting them toward the children's peer groups.[17]

The relationships that Americans have with their groups reveal contradictory qualities. We join groups when membership suits our needs; we leave when it doesn't. We're fine with the togetherness that membership entails, but we can't even imagine relinquishing our unique identities and decision-making autonomy. We see ourselves as free to disagree, to push our own agendas. We bridle if others see us as "compliant." Such feelings are examples of how our commitment to individualism shapes our feelings and behavior in daily life.

For most Japanese, expressions of personal autonomy and uniqueness vis-à-vis the other members of one's group are not appropriate. In this section, we'll explore how teachers at the preschool and early primary levels help youngsters gradually learn how to live the Japanese way.

Two Types of Groups in Japanese Society

The Japanese term for an important group in one's life, but not one's family, is *shūdan seikatsu*. (*Shūdan* is a human collective; *seikatsu* is daily living.) The difference between such a group and a family is not the number of members but the expectations about their behavior.

In their homes, adults and children expect intimacy and indulgence, with fathers and children being especially dependent on the mother. Family members may behave pretty much as they please, indulging their desires. In this warm environment, everyone may use a communication style called *honne* (literally, "true sound"), sharing their feelings and speaking their minds. Communication that is *honne* also is acceptable, even expected, within a group of longtime close friends.

But beyond home, family, and one's intimate friends, a distinct social tendency toward *tatemae* prevails. Communication and behavior that is *tatemae* requires the individual, regardless of his or her own momentary feelings and needs, to make harmony within the group a priority. Expected are diligent efforts to maintain a pleasant social atmosphere, subtle probing of the ideas and opinions of others, and empathetic attunement to others' expressed and, more significantly, unexpressed feelings. Pushing one's own ideas or agenda is not done. One mother described her daughter as adopting *tatemae* expectations by saying that her child is now "keeping her wings pulled in."[18]

Another way of distinguishing between these two concepts is to equate *honne* with one's true inner voice. *Tatemae* is usefully equated with one's public stance on an issue, or with one's putting up a front, that is, putting up an external appearance in order to be socially tactful and mindful of others' sensibilities.[19]

Preschool is where children are initiated into the *tatemae* realm. In addition to being helped to gradually adopt the *tatemae* way of behaving, they also are coached to learn how to detect situational changes between *honne* and *tatemae*, and then adapt their own behavior to complement that of other group members. The skill of discerning the appropriate behavior to be exhibited at a given time, and then of switching quickly to the desirable mode, is known as *kejime*.[20]

A Japanese researcher said about *shūdan seikatsu* living that the key value holding such a group together is "voluntary cooperation with a heavy dose of empathy," adding that "voluntary" is not the American if-you'd-like-to-variety but an intentionally developed mindset.[21]

How do preschool and early primary teachers instill this mindset?

Learning to Loathe Loneliness

It's likely that emotions are more often expressed and discussed in Japanese preschools than in American ones. The emotion most often referenced is that of feeling *sabishii*, meaning lonely and sad.[22] This is not because the children come to school feeling lonely. Rather, it's because teachers look for ways to remind youngsters that loneliness is a feeling that one should help others avoid by encouraging and helping them to become active group members.

Researchers report that they often witnessed teachers talking with pupils about the feelings of other people—and of animals, plants, even objects. Most often, loneliness was the topic.

A teacher stands in front of her class of four-year-olds and holds up brightly colored sheets of origami paper. "We're going to make fish today. [She demonstrates and explains] And one more fold, like this. Got it? Good! Now it looks like a fish. But it looks so *sabishii* without a mouth or eyes. What should we do?"

At lunchtime, a teacher notices that many of the children have left their carrots untouched. Speaking to a boy in a theatrical voice loud enough for the whole class to hear, she says, "Poor Mister Carrot! You ate Mr. Hamburger, Mr. Rice, and Mr. Orange, but you haven't eaten any of Mr. Carrot. Don't you think he feels *sabishii*?"[23]

Two aspects of these teachers' statements are important. First, they are helping the children develop a robust notion of the possibility, and the undesirability, of loneliness and sadness. More significant is that neither the origami fish nor the carrots have given any observable sign that they're feeling lonely and sad. The teachers are demonstrating how one can be alert to sense someone's (or something's) *unexpressed* feeling, then respond to it in an empathetic way that alleviates the individual's loneliness while preserving the group's harmony.

If you've read much about the Japanese, you might have come across the word *amae*, often discussed in relation to a child's relationship with his mother. *Amae*, sometimes translated as "longing," means making someone want to care for you.[24] You behave in such a way that your need to be with and depend on him or her is clear, *ideally without your asking*. The other person, sensing your longing for connection, is likely to respond empathetically and positively—called *omoiyari* in Japanese.

Preschool and primary teachers apply a three-step process:

1. *Sabishii*—Children are made aware of the undesirability of anyone or even anything being left out and feeling lonely and therefore sad.
2. *Amae*—Children are encouraged to long for togetherness with and dependence on their peers, and to express this, ideally nonverbally.
3. *Omoiyari*—Children sense, naturally or with coaching, a peer's longing for inclusion, and respond with empathy and warm acceptance.[25]

In this way, a "pedagogy of feeling" plays a key role in guiding children to form warmly cohesive groups and treat them as central to their lives.

TYPES OF JAPANESE PRESCHOOLS

The type of preschool described in this chapter and the next was very common in Japan during the period 1985–2010 when most preschool research was carried out. But it was not, and still is not, the only type. One researcher who documented the variety of preschools came to the conclusion that there are three main types.[26]

1. **Relationship-oriented.** This is the type of preschool described in this chapter and the following one. Its main characteristic is the goal of preparing children for participation in group life via long periods of free play that engender spontaneous friendships, which help to stimulate strong group identification. Emphasis is placed on the children's learning to resolve their own issues, even to the point of the teachers' deliberately shorting craft and play materials so as to induce conflict. Also very important are (a) encouraging children to sense others' feelings and needs and to respond with empathy and (b) training them to sense shifts in social situations and switch (*kejime*) their behavior accordingly. Large class sizes are typical. Many public and private schools are of the relationship-oriented type.

2. **Child-oriented.** This preschool type originated in part due to the interest of some Japanese in progressive education. Child-centered schools feature small class sizes and much free play. Craft and play materials rarely are shorted; staff insure that whatever children want is available. Teachers spend much time in one-on-one interactions with individual children, made practical by small class sizes. Each child is helped to identify his or her personal interests, needs, and feelings, and to openly express them to peers. Teachers see themselves as fostering good social relationships through enabling each child to express his own perspective during social interactions, including fights. Child-oriented preschools appeal mainly to wealthy parents. Some are operated by Roman Catholics and other mainstream Christian groups,[27] but others are public.

3. **Role-oriented or academic.** Driving this type are traditional Japanese values holding that self-discipline, persevering effort, and endurance of hardship are paths to human excellence. They have been called *role*-oriented because they view their mission as preparing children "to perform their role in life with diligence, confidence, and competence." The ethic underlying these schools might seem to be simply self-denial and compliance. But the teachers see themselves as building children's character and academic skills, as well as strengthening their weaknesses, in a highly structured environment that expects diligent effort. There is constant direct instruction in math, reading, art, gymnastics, and more. There's no free play and no opportunity for peer-to-peer interaction except during lunch. Punishments do occur, including isolation. Such preschools are popular with working-class parents who want their children to have a head start in primary school. Many are run by Buddhist groups.[28]

A MIRROR FOR AMERICANS

As we Americans look into the mirror provided by East Asian preschool education, what do we notice about *our* schools—and about the concepts and values *we* apply when thinking about schools?

- **The learning of social skills:** Several methods for ingraining social skills in Japanese preschoolers have been depicted in this chapter. Contrasts with our American ways include that there is far more emphasis on group cohesion and far greater reliance on children's experiential learning of social skills. Precept, example, and intervention also occur. But the extent to which Japanese preschoolers are expected to figure out how to resolve their disputes is stunning—not to mention that play materials are intentionally short-supplied to add occasions for them to do so.

  At the level of core values about how to comport oneself in society, the contrasts between Japan and the United States are enormous. Clearly, our me-me-me culture is not fertile ground for the Japanese approach to insuring that preschoolers learn how to live with others. And if we did seriously attempt to replicate their ways, a parental uproar would surely follow.

- **Extent of freedom allowed:** During their lengthy free play periods, Japanese preschoolers are routinely allowed the run of the entire school and its grounds with virtually no supervision and are often left to deal with disagreements on their own. Words such as "freedom" and "self-reliance" seem applicable to these practices. By whatever name, there's plenty of it!

  Therein lies a paradox: We Americans wax passionate about inculcating in our children self-reliance, self-control, self-confidence, and other attributes of "freedom." But when we consider our ways while looking into the mirror of Japanese preschool practices, we become conscious that we're monitoring and restricting our youngsters' movements, protecting them from every possible risk, rushing to intervene in their childish disputes, and insisting that they choose from among a handful of adult-devised activity centers during free play. Do these practices instill self-reliance, self-control, and self-confidence?

- **Individual- or group-emphasis**: The East Asian mirror reminds us that our early childhood programs are influenced from top to bottom by our hallowed value of individualism. It's not that we disapprove of empathy and harmony among children in groups.[29] We're warmly in favor of all that—so long as group attachments do nothing to undermine each child's developing self-acceptance, self-confidence, self-expressiveness, self-reliance, self-assertiveness, creativity, and proud appreciation of his or her own unique qualities and abilities.

Neither individual nor group orientation, *by itself*, has a significant effect on the quality or quantity of students' academic learning. The reason why this chapter is devoted to group orientation is that it's a basic building block of Japanese classroom learning, and thus, a prerequisite for understanding the following chapter, "East Asian Preschools II: Where Children Learn How to Learn."

FURTHER READING

If you'd like more detail about the researchers' findings, or simply wish to know what inspired the contents of chapter 2, read the following entries in the annotated bibliography at www.amirrorforamericans.info.

- Ben-Ari, Eyal (1997), *Body Projects in Japanese Childcare.*
- Che, Yi, Akiko Hayashi, & Joseph Tobin (2007), Lessons from China and Japan for preschool practice in the United States.
- Hayashi, Akiko, Mayumi Karasawa, & Joseph Tobin (2009), The Japanese preschool's pedagogy of feeling.
- Hendry, Joy (1986), *Becoming Japanese: The World of the Pre-school Child.*
- Hoffman, Diane M. (2000), Individualism and individuality in American and Japanese early education.
- Holloway, Susan D. (2000), *Contested Childhood: Diversity and Change in Japanese Preschools.*
- Lewis, Catherine (1991), Nursery schools: The transition from home to school.
- Lewis, Catherine C. (1995), *Educating Hearts and Minds.*
- Orlick, Terry, Qi-ying Zhou, & John Partington (1990), Co-operation and conflict within Chinese and Canadian kindergarten settings.
- Peak, Lois (1991a), *Learning to Go to School in Japan.*
- Tobin, Joseph, Yeh Hsueh, & Mayumi Karasawa (2009b), Chapter 3: Japan. *Preschool in Three Cultures Revisited.*
- Tobin, Joseph J., David Y. H. Wu, & Dana H. Davidson (1991), Forming groups.
- Tsuneyoshi, Ryoko (2001), *The Japanese Model of Schooling.*

Chapter 3

East Asian Preschools, Part II
Where Children Learn How to Learn

The goal of education is the reduction of individual differences among children.

Japanese education official[1]

David Lancy is a scholar who collects and analyzes the works of anthropologists, historians, and others who explore how children are raised and socialized in all documented cultures, past and present. Based on his encyclopedic command of childhood research, Dr. Lancy tells us that:

• Schools aren't necessary. In all known cultures, children become functioning members of society whether or not they were schooled.
• In cultures with formal schooling, children invariably resist it because it requires them to curb their exuberance. They must be "tamed."
• There are two ways of taming young learners: Either their resistance is *overcome* via carrot or stick or it is *prevented* from occurring.[2]

In the United States, children's resistance is largely *overcome*. In past times, resistance was overcome via the stick. Nowadays it's all about the carrot. The learning environment is made appealing—schools are inviting, lessons are fun—in hopes that children will become engaged.

In East Asia, a child's resistance is largely *prevented* through the fostering of an "adaptive disposition."[3] Both parents and teachers contribute to this shaping of the child's attitudes about school learning.

Infants and small children everywhere absorb the values and attitudes characteristic of their local culture from their parents, other children, extended family, and other older people in their lives. As explained in *The Drive to Learn*, the outcome in East Asia is that children arrive at the schoolhouse door "more receptive to classroom learning," and with a greater disposition to adapt to it, than their American peers do.

In this chapter, we'll explore how children's adaptive dispositions are fostered by preschool teachers in East Asia. Like parents, they play a role in preventing children's resistance to learning in school by guiding them *to learn how to learn*, that is, to gradually acquire attitudes and activities that facilitate learning in classrooms.

To understand this, we need to first become familiar with one of the traditional—and up-to-date—themes of the Japanese culture of learning.

KATA AS THE ENTRY POINT FOR SCHOOLING

If you've ever learned a Japanese martial art—*karate, aikidō, jūdō*, and so on—or tea ceremony or flower arrangement, you'll likely have heard of the concept of *kata*. Literally translated as "form," it also can function as a suffix of any Japanese verb, where it means "way of doing" in the sense of an established orderly process. In the martial arts, kata refers to a finely choreographed pattern of precise physical movements that a learner practices and absorbs into his neural and muscular systems.

Kata isn't just some ancient notion prettied up to appeal to modern folks. Today, the kata concept is turning up in mainstream business thinking. Here's how an American-made website discusses how the application of kata can be used for improving oneself and/or one's workgroup:

> Brain scientists like to say, "Anytime you do something you're more likely to do it again." In other words, thoughts and behaviors that we repeat, intentionally or unintentionally, can get woven into the neural structures of our brain. From sports and music, we know that these ingredients develop new skills and habits: (1) structured routines for beginners to practice, (2) frequent repetition, (3) feedback from a coach to correct our practice, (4) optimism and enthusiasm.[4]

The objective of repetitive practice is not only to learn to perform certain movements and techniques correctly, but also to gain the ability to do so in a natural, reflex-like manner. Repetitive practice ingrains the movements of the kata in mental and muscle memory so they can be carried out smoothly without thought, even in novel circumstances. This repetitive process for learning something new is called "entering through form."[5]

In addition to the Japanese emphasis on kata, the idea is held among many in East Asia that, across millennia, wise scholars and skillful artists have honed to perfection the basics of learning anything that's worth knowing. So if something must be learned, a novice should seek active guidance and unsparing critiques by someone—a "master"—who already has worked long and hard to perfect it.

Kata for Kindergarten Kids?

Kata isn't only for kindergarten kids; it's for preschool kids, too.[6] And for Japanese children, it begins on their very first day at school.

In all nations with early childhood programs, preschool teachers face the challenge of dealing with tiny youngsters for whom a classroom is utterly new and strange. Clearly, some semblance of order needs to be established during the fledglings' early weeks. But how teachers in East Asia conceive of "classroom order," and the ways they expect to establish it, are unlike our American approaches.

In Japan, the difference isn't merely about pedagogical practices. It's about a fundamental orientation to all of life and learning:

There's a right way to do something that everyone must master.[7]

This concept informs preschool teachers' thinking about classroom order and how they establish it. The little ones are facing a wholly new situation, so their teachers will shepherd them to *enter it through form.* The process is gradual: two steps forward, one step back. The teachers are patient but also persistent—gentle persuasion relentlessly applied.

On children's first day at school, and every day thereafter when they arrive at school hand-in-hand with their mothers, they encounter the child's waiting teacher. There's a *right* way to greet one's teacher:

> As child and mother come within speaking distance of the teacher, they make the first move. Coming to a full halt with both feet together and hands in front, child and mother bow, inclining their heads from three to six inches, and loudly announce in standard formal language, "Good morning, Teacher." The teacher smiles in recognition and returns the greeting and bow.[8]

To Westerners, this greeting might seem formal and ritualistic, even unfriendly. That's due to an East-West cultural contrast: In the United States, *informal* speech and behavior conveys positive regard for another because it signals *friendly.* We don't like rituals because we associate them with lack of spontaneity and warmth. But in East Asia, *formal* speech and behavior conveys warmth and positive regard for another because it signals *respectful.* People in East Asia expect and appreciate rituals because they pave the way to congenial relationships with others.

Of course, on their first day at school, new pupils won't know the kata for greeting a teacher. No problem! Adults will help the child get it right, patiently modeling how to do it during each day's arrival.[9]

"Entering through Form" for New Preschoolers

How to greet a teacher is just the first skill for the neophytes to master. There are many more *how-to* routines to be learned in the classroom.

> The child proceeds to the classroom to put away his belongings and change clothes. After removing and hanging up his traveling smock, shoulder bag, and traveling hat, he puts on his play smock and play hat. When he has stacked his parent-teacher message book on the teacher's desk, he is free to run about and play.
>
> Changing clothing and organizing materials on arrival is one of the many basic habits of daily life that Japanese preschools take great pains to inculcate in students. The habits will be further elaborated in elementary school and will remain with the children throughout life.[10]

Different preschools have different morning routines. In many cases, pupils formally assemble after they've all arrived. Here's an account from one preschool of what happens then:

> The day begins proper when the teacher plays a melody on the piano. It is the same tune each day and the signal for the children to sit down in a circle. They should clasp their knees and remain quiet until all are seated. The teacher plays the same tune until everyone complies. Once they are ready, she breaks into a contrasting drill that is the new signal for everyone to jump to their feet. It is followed by a cadence to which they all bow nicely, after which she plays the good morning song, which has been practiced until it becomes an automatic response. It is the same song each morning so everyone joins in with great gusto. The teacher says "good morning" and the children chorus their reply.[11]

There's a huge gulf separating the free play described in the previous chapter—an unregimented, unsupervised, uninhibited, and wholly without "form" period—and the scenes depicted above of an orderly, ritualized, *formal* daily ceremony that's been practiced to mastery. Are chapters 2 and 3 talking about two different types of preschools?

No. It's all in pursuit of the aforementioned value: *the youngsters will gain an active sense of community*. Solidifying this in young hearts and minds is a combination of three activities: unrestrained free play, choreographed group behavior, and reflection (*hansei*), which we'll discuss later in this chapter. There are other choreographed activities, too. Each is part of the kata of attending school. Preschool is where the children are coaxed and coached to enter it all "through form."

KATA AS THE ENTRY POINT FOR LEARNING

Western observers visiting Japanese upper-elementary classrooms are aston-
ished by the effortless efficiency with which teachers conduct lessons. Students transition from one activity to another—sometimes rearranging the
furniture—as though they were a single organism; yet merely one sentence
spoken by their teacher prompted them to do so—for example, "Get into your
four-person groups." Work in small groups proceeds smoothly, with students
ably filling roles such as leader and recorder. Whole-class instruction is
business-like because the children observe routinized procedures for presenting, asking, and answering questions, and so forth. And it's all accomplished
without tight authoritarian control.[12]

Japanese upper-elementary classrooms are characterized by learning processes that proceed smoothly and effectively because when those youngsters
were in preschool and first grade, they were intentionally taught *how to
actively contribute to efficient classroom learning.*

During the early grades, pupils are explicitly taught, then practice *practice
practice,* the correct ways of greeting their teacher, of arranging items both *on*
and *inside* their desks, and of sitting with backs straight, hands on knees, eyes
focused forward. They learn and practice the proper way to sit while studying, to raise one hand to signal a public contribution, to stand to speak, and to
come to the front of the room and publicly present their ideas (such as a math
solution). They learn to rearrange a room for small group meetings and how
to again make it suitable for whole-group instruction. These highly efficient
classroom learning routines have been termed "learner-trained learning."[13]

> As children become more adept at setting up the room, teachers gradually
> withdraw almost completely from the setting-up process. They prefer to allow
> children to learn how to organize themselves and work together, even at the
> expense of extra time and some confusion.
>
> Every routine basic to daily classroom life is broken down into a series of
> careful steps, painstakingly practiced again and again until it becomes second
> nature, and then speeded up until it becomes an automatic, smoothly executed
> part of the school day, accomplished with the speed and assurance of a drill
> team.[14]

When there are well-rehearsed, largely choreographed templates for each
of the activities necessary for any classroom lesson to proceed efficiently,
teachers need not issue complex instructions nor monitor how well they're
being followed. *Teacher and students can direct the vast majority of their
attention to the new material to be learned.*

One researcher estimated that, compared with American teachers, Japanese
teachers are able to spend almost 50 percent more time per classroom period
imparting subject content.[15]

Learning to Share Responsibility for Effective Classroom Learning

Who is responsible for each student's learning? When this is asked comparatively about schooling in two or more nations, the answers often expose deep cultural contrasts.

Here's an example from our own nation. In August 2016, the "Commentary" section of *Education Week* featured an opinion piece by a retired school superintendent who is on the faculty of a graduate school of education. The article's title was, "Who Should Be Responsible for Student Learning?" In answering his own question, the author mentions state graduation standards, No Child Left Behind, the Common Core, teachers unions, charter schools, family poverty, and teacher-related factors such as certification, accountability, and tenure.[16]

That's a long list! Surely, no potentially responsible person or entity has been overlooked.

But if you're Japanese, you notice a significant omission: the pupils. That's because after their preschool and early grade training, Japanese pupils know how to supportively participate in classroom learning. They've practiced the physical moves and the roles and routines. They've often attained the desired outcomes of their individual and collective efforts. So from now on, *the pupils themselves share some of the responsibility for their own effective learning.*

Furthermore, the teacher's stance vis-à-vis her pupils can become non-authoritarian. She rarely needs to issue detailed instructions about any activity related to the progress of a lesson. It's all been fine-tuned and practiced repeatedly. She needs only to state the nature of the next learning activity, relying on her pupils to efficiently make her request a reality.[17]

One researcher cited the example of the Suzuki piano-teaching method. Novices repeatedly rehearse actions such as reacting to the teacher's entrance, arranging items on a desktop, and sitting properly. They are coached to precisely execute movements such as orienting the body, using the hands, and focusing the gaze. Is the teacher being authoritative? Yes. But after it's all become internalized, the need for further detailed directives from the teacher is slight:

> The tiny child responds quickly and accurately to the teacher's instructions, with eyes never leaving the keyboard. The lesson is surprisingly businesslike, with a minimum of fun and games and sugar-coated sweetness. The enjoyment the child derives is the personal satisfaction of competent execution and growing ability.[18]

You could think of it this way: training small children to learn *how to learn* infuses classroom procedures with *mindfulness*, not merely on the part of the teacher but also on the part of her pupils. Speed in task performance is actively deemphasized in favor of extreme care and precision. Sloppy execution is always remedied.[19]

Perhaps you're wondering why we've explored only the youngsters' learning *how* to learn, ignoring the process by which they actually begin learning academic material. One reason is this: Ministry of Education guidelines explicitly discourage academic learning in preschools.[20]

TEACHERS' RELATIONSHIPS WITH THEIR PUPILS

In chapter 2, we discussed the "pedagogy of feeling" that characterizes Japanese preschools. Preschools are where Japanese youngsters are initiated into Japanese ways for participating wholeheartedly in a non-family group. The key value holding such a group together is "voluntary cooperation with a heavy dose of empathy."

Preschool teachers guide their young charges to adopt these ways of life. The relationships teachers build with their pupils have fascinated researchers, whose findings we will explore under these headings:

- Teachers strive to "touch the children's hearts."
- Teachers mute authority and maintain a low profile.
- Children help to shape classroom norms.
- Children rotate in the class leadership role.
- Periods of reflection evaluate self and group.

Teachers Strive to "Touch the Children's Hearts"

For Japanese teachers who will work at the preschool and early grade levels, teacher training instills a mindset and spirit that strongly prioritizes their developing close, intimate connections with their pupils.[21] A Japanese word that's sometimes applied is *kizuna*, which in this case refers to a relationship fostering empathy and "a touching of the hearts."[22]

New teachers aren't specifically advised to insure that their authority is recognized. In Western cultures, maintaining authority typically requires objectivity and emotional distance, the opposite of what works in Japan. *Kizuna* isn't about children's compliance, but about instilling in them feelings of security, commitment, and trust.

In chapter 2 we reviewed the concept of *amae*. A similar quality, one that values deep attachment and dependency, applies to teacher-pupil relations. A handbook prepared by a school district for new teachers put it like this:

To become a teacher trusted by the students, he/she must fully know the fears, worries, and aspirations of each child and deliberately and effectively plan ways to deal with the problems children have. By doing this, the teacher will promote children's confidence in him/her.[23]

During an interview, a teacher-in-training within that district said:

> To gain my students' confidence in me, I have to sweat with them. I think that trustful relationships will develop when I, as a teacher, let my children see me do all I can in my encounters with them, joining them in whatever they are doing.[24]

In pursuit of that objective, that teacher-in-training began participating in an annual practice of all Japanese elementary teachers: he visited every student's home to familiarize himself with the parents' perspectives on their child.

Teachers Mute Authority and Maintain a Low Profile

A mindset of "monitor and control" is foreign to Japanese teachers. We've already seen how preschool teachers refrain from being the arbiters of good and bad. In addition, when the class has a discussion, the teacher serves as a resource, not as the leader. She encourages pupils to justify their comments, reconcile them with others' views, or relate them to the overarching goal of building their community.[25]

Teachers don't issue commands. The ways in which they gently and gradually steer the children to observe community norms include:[26]

- **Modeling correct behavior:** A demonstration by the teacher is given in some cases; more often an assistant teacher ostentatiously models the right way to behave. Ideal, of course, is when a *child* can be pointed to as the model.

- **Reacting to misbehavior by discussing feelings:** When a child does something undesirable, teachers don't react by referencing a rule. They cite its disagreeable effect on the group or a classmate. "How would Ryoko have felt if that block you threw had hit her?"

- **Reminding and guiding:** Teachers remind and assist individuals who haven't yet mastered a certain behavior. They never show impatience, never punish or isolate. Sometimes after a very young child has been reminded several times, the teacher will simply drop it.

- **Seconding children's requests:** When one or more pupils spontaneously call for classmates to do the right thing, the teacher will agree. Child: "Shut up!" Teacher: "Yes, let's all be quiet."[27]

- **Keeping the entire class waiting:** We've already encountered this in chapter 2. It might seem an exercise in the teacher's authority, but it's always related to promoting the unity of all class members.

When a child finally manages to do things right, he or she is praised as *jōzu*, "skillful," implying effort. Rarely will a newly performing child be praised as "good," implying that he's stopped being "bad."[28] A child who violates group norms is said to have "forgotten his promises" or "not understood." Misbehavior is labeled "strange" or "odd."[29]

Children Help to Shape Classroom Norms

A classroom needs some routines and rules to function smoothly.[30] In Japanese preschools and the first years of primary schools, teachers insure that these arise "naturally," meaning that they come from the children. Such matters aren't discussed until the second or third month, after children have "bumped up against one another" and appreciate the usefulness of rules— "promises" arising from empathy and thoughtful concern for everyone's well-being. There's no schedule for this; it's never rushed. Teachers sometimes keep hinting for weeks, patiently waiting for the youngsters to notice that such-and-such a chore needs doing.

> Several months into the year, everyone talked about the need for someone to do chores, so the idea emerged of taking turns. Now the monitors come back to the classroom early from outside and do the work without my saying a word. They open windows, pass out the straws, and wipe the tables. At the end of the day, the children have a "baton touch" and transfer authority to the next day's monitors.[31]

Children Rotate in the Class Leadership Role[32]

In Japanese preschool classrooms, the role of student monitor—*tōban*—is rotated from day to day so that *every* child serves. Student leadership is never conferred because of one's popularity, skillful performance, or exemplary behavior.

A *tōban* might lead daily calisthenics, decide when the class is quiet enough for the next activity to begin, pass out art materials, inspect lunchboxes, or even decide when to dismiss individual children to play outside. By the first grade, *tōban* chair meetings, evaluate other pupils' behavior, lead efforts to solve disputes, and manage other processes.

In some classes, the next day's *tōban* is designated with a formal ceremony. Both teachers and pupils add the honorific -*san* to his or her surname (e.g., Nakamura-san) and bow. But because *tōban* actually have key responsibilities for the smooth progress of the day, those who fall down on the job become the targets of their classmates' disappointment ("Hey, where are our snacks?"). Teachers are reluctant to compensate for a *tōban*'s over-sight. In one documented instance, a classmate walloped an errant *tōban*, who protested to the teacher. The teacher's response was, "He hit you because you forgot your job."[33]

Periods of Reflection Evaluate Self and Group

The belief that it's valuable to pause and mindfully reflect on events in one's environment and the quality of one's contribution to them is a constant in Japanese life, practiced as a group process as well as individually by people of all ages. Reflection has spiritual and aesthetic qualities as well as practical outcomes: think of tea ceremony, flower arranging, calligraphy, martial arts, and meditation.[34]

You might be familiar with *kaizen*, the Japanese ideal of continually striving to attain perfection in process and product. It is closely related to the practice of reflection, termed *hansei*, because its purpose is to contemplate ways in which a group's life and work can be perfected, and what one needs to do better to contribute to that end.[35]

Preschool is where most Japanese youngsters begin the practice of *hansei*. It occurs at least once daily near day's end, sometimes more often. It's never rushed. One researcher has written extensively about *hansei* at the preschool and early elementary levels:

> Students didn't just *do* chores; they reflect on them. Had everyone helped? Were class animals and property being cared for well? What should children do when classmates shirked chores? Children often recognized the quiet, slow workers who had plugged away at chores even as their more gregarious groupmates became distracted.
>
> Incidents of fighting or dangerous behavior resurfaced. Teachers made community property out of incidents such as two boys' fistfight over a wrecked sand castle. Teachers bent over backward to describe sympathetically each child's reasons for fighting. As they explored the feelings that led to conflicts and the attempts of classmates to help solve them, teachers made clear that the responsibility for solving problems belongs to the entire class.
>
> The aim of reflection went beyond social skills to the values children brought to group life and the strength of children's bonds to one another. As one teacher said, children's "whole way of looking at one another changed" as they reflected on help and kindness offered by classmates.
>
> *Because of the time and care devoted to these discussions, I came to see them as the real curriculum of Japanese preschools. Free play, with its conflicts and kindnesses, provided the grist for this curriculum.*[36]

A GLIMPSE AT CHINESE PRESCHOOLS[37]

During the 1990s, the Chinese government proclaimed "Education for Quality" as its policy and pushed for significant changes in classroom teaching that reflected Western "progressive" ideas, many of which had been introduced to China around 1920 by John Dewey himself.[38] Under the new policy, child-centered approaches were meant to nurture self-assertion and creativity, and academic subjects were deemphasized. These initiatives sparked pushback from many parents and teachers.

Like their Japanese peers, Chinese preschoolers are taught *how to learn.* They acquire attentive attitudes, coordinated physical movements, and ways of working with peers so that, in subsequent years, they can enable classroom time to be used almost 100 percent for learning.[39]

Four ways in which Chinese preschools differ from those of Japan, as suggested by research reports, are these:

• Chinese preschool classrooms are more structured than those in Japan; teachers are more likely to introduce academic topics using both traditional and progressive methods.[40]

• Long periods of unrestrained, unsupervised free play aren't common in China. Play is more likely to involve a variety of teacher-organized and -monitored activities.[41]

• It's rare in China for teachers to ignore bad behavior and fights; they are far more likely to get involved, at least by making suggestions. Teachers are more likely to expect disciplined, quiet children.[42]

• Chinese preschoolers are encouraged to openly evaluate their classmates' performances, and to listen calmly as classmates evaluate theirs. This contrasts with the encouragement of Japanese preschoolers to openly share how they could improve *themselves* and become more responsive to others' unstated feelings. (American preschoolers are encouraged to talk openly about their *own* feelings. To enhance their self-esteem, they rarely receive any public evaluation other than praise.)[43]

After describing kindergarten classrooms in which the Chinese language was being taught in two Chinese cities, two researchers offered this summary:

> In classes for maths, music, art, or dance, a similar approach prevails: The teacher instructs from the front; she presents careful clear models for the children; she shows them what to learn and how to learn it; the learners all perform the same tasks at the same time; there is clear discipline, uniform attention

and concentration, punctuated by varied activities. As we talk to teachers in different schools they repeatedly emphasize conforming and cooperation; communication and confidence; and meaningful models and memorization through analysis, step-by-step repetition, reproduction, and recitation. In this culture of learning there is great consistency.[44]

A MIRROR FOR AMERICANS

As we Americans look into the mirror provided by East Asian preschool education, what do we notice about our schools—and about the concepts and values we apply when thinking about schools?

- **Organizing classroom learning:** By looking into the mirror of Japanese preschools, where the teachers' goal is *to reduce children's individual differences*, we become conscious of the extent to which American teachers preserve pupils' freedom to display their special qualities—not only as unique individuals but also as members of families and other significant groups in their lives.

  In Japan, the goal of reducing individual differences is put into the service of efficient classroom processes. The means to this end is the concept of "entering through form": as a group, pupils *practice to mastery* the elements of effective classroom process so that, during their ensuing years in classrooms, they will on cue (or even uncued) perform those elements swiftly and accurately. Countless hours are thereby freed for productive teaching and learning.

  In my view, the kata for classroom learning—also instilled by schools other than those that are relationship-oriented—is one of the factors that gives Japanese students a competitive edge as they move on to study other academic subjects, and thereby helps to account for their superior performances on the international tests.

- **Teachers' wielding of authority:** Anthropological accounts of daily activities in relationship-oriented Japanese preschools portray the teachers as (a) making light use of the authority that is inherently theirs, (b) building relationships with the children characterized by a "touching of the hearts," and (c) encouraging relationships among the children that involve emotional connections and empathy. Every account marvels at how teachers slowly shift responsibility for the group's smooth functioning to the pupils, which makes it ever less necessary for the teachers to even *think* of asserting their authority.

The contrast with American teachers' approach is sharp: here, there are oceans of warmth and friendliness to go around, but they come with the tacit—sometimes explicit—message that "I am responsible for your safety and learning, so I will monitor and direct you in this class."

Hold on! Aren't American schools supposed to be child-centered?

FURTHER READING

If you'd like more detail about the researchers' findings, or simply wish to know what inspired the contents of chapter 3, read these entries in the annotated bibliography at www.amirrorforamericans.info.

- Che, Yi, Akiko Hayashi, & Joseph Tobin (2007), Lessons from China and Japan for preschool practice in the United States.
- Davin, Delia (1991), The early childhood education of the only-child generation in urban China.
- Hendry, Joy (1986), *Becoming Japanese: The World of the Pre-school Child*.
- Hess, Robert D., & Hiroshi Azuma (1991), Cultural support for schooling.
- Lewis, Catherine (1991), Nursery schools: The transition from home to school.
- Lewis, Catherine C. (1995), *Educating Hearts and Minds: Reflections on Japanese Preschool and Elementary Education*.
- Li, Hui, X. Christine Wang, & Jessie Ming Sin Wong (2011), Early childhood curriculum reform in China.
- Peak, Lois (1991a), *Learning to Go to School in Japan*.
- Peak, Lois (1991b), Training learning skills and attitudes in Japanese early education settings.
- Rohlen, Thomas P., & Gerald K. LeTendre (1998), Conclusion: Themes in the Japanese culture of learning.
- Sato, Nancy E. (2004), *Inside Japanese Classrooms: The Heart of Education*.
- Shimahara, Nobuo K., & Akira Sakai (1995), *Learning to Teach in Two Cultures*.
- Singleton, John (1991), The spirit of *gambaru*.
- Stevenson, Harold W., & James W. Stigler (1992), *The Learning Gap*.
- Stimpfl, Joseph, Fuming Zheng, & William Meredith (1997), A garden in the motherland: A study of a preschool in China.

- Tobin, Joseph, David Y.H. Wu, & Dana H. Davidson (1991), Forming groups.
- Tobin, Joseph, Yeh Hsueh, & Mayumi Karasawa (2009b), Chapter 3: Japan. *Preschool in Three Cultures Revisited.*
- Tsuchida, Ineko, & Catherine C. Lewis (1998), Responsibility and learning: Some preliminary hypotheses about Japanese elementary classrooms.
- Tsuneyoshi, Ryoko (2001), *The Japanese Model of Schooling.*

Two recently published nonfiction books offer insights, from a mother's perspective, on early primary school education in contemporary China and Japan. In both cases the child is not native-born, the mother is a journalist with ties to the U.S., and the school is "elite" in the sense that it caters to parents and children from society's top echelons. Each book illuminates the experiences of both the child and the mother. Both books are included in the online annotated bibliography.

- Chu, Lenora (2017), *Little Soldiers: An American Boy, a Chinese School, and the Global Race to Achieve.* Harper, 347 pages.
- Makihara, Kumiko (2018), *Dear Diary Boy: An Exacting Mother, Her Free-Spirited Son, and Their Bittersweet Adventures in an Elite Japanese School.* Arcade, 218 pages.

Chapter 4

Foundations of East Asian Schooling, Part I

How Children's Learning Is Regarded

I had paid little attention to the society's stake in exposing all students to certain basic ideas, principles, and facts.

Howard Gardner, after visiting
primary schools in China[1]

More is occurring in any classroom than the transmission of items of skill or knowledge. A classroom is populated day after day with young people who, in addition to learning math, reading, and so on, are facing the prospect of becoming contributing members of the society they find themselves inhabiting. Their classroom is overseen by an older person who, like the parents of most of the pupils, has years of experience internalizing that society's assumptions, values, and expectations.

In this chapter we'll explore how people in East Asia think about learning. We'll pay special attention to their assumptions, values, and expectations regarding learning-related attitudes and behavior.

THINKING OF LEARNING

What comes into a person's mind when he or she thinks about "learning" or "to learn" depends on the culture in which that person was raised. One scholar explored what comes to mind when American and Chinese people think about learning.[2] As summarized by Table 4.1, she found that

When thinking of learning, **Americans** have in mind

- processes (study, thinking, reading, discovery),
- places and things (school, library, books, brain),
- concepts (understand, knowledge, motivation),

- roles (teacher, students),
- knowledge as a *neutral* body of information that an individual's mind should acquire because it might be personally useful in the future.

When thinking of learning, **Chinese** people have in mind

- strong desire and passion for knowing,
- hard work, perseverance, and discipline,
- learning challenges that must be overcome,
- constantly learning throughout one's entire life,
- knowledge as the *emotionally charged* basis for perfecting oneself as a person who contributes to the well-being of his family and other groups.

Table 4.1   What comes to mind when they think about "learning"?

AMERICANS	CHINESE
Thoughts related to one's mind	Thoughts related to one's heart
Upgrading one's practical capabilities	Perfecting oneself as a human being
Worthwhile for me in the future	Worthwhile for my group right away
Neutral characteristics and processes	Emotional passion and commitment
A really good idea; maybe interesting, too	Resolve; disciplined, persevering effort
A process with a beginning and an end	A lifelong quest for self-perfection

Source: Jin Li (2012). *Cultural Foundations of Learning: East and West*. Based on findings reported in chapter 3.

Virtue as a Component of Learning

David Brooks is a public intellectual whose columns appear in *The New York Times*. One of Brooks's columns asked what it means to be a good person. He wrote that it had occurred to him

> that there are two sets of virtues, the résumé virtues and the eulogy virtues. The résumé virtues are the skills you bring to the marketplace. The eulogy virtues are the ones that are talked about at your funeral—whether you were kind, brave, honest, or faithful.[3]

Note first that Brooks spoke of "virtues." That word rarely occurs in discussions of American education, but it turns up often in discussions about East Asian pre- and primary school education. When people in East Asia think about educating their young, one of their main objectives is to inculcate *virtue* (as they understand it, of course).

The distinction between *résumé virtues* and *eulogy virtues* is useful in answering the question about what comes into the minds of people in the United States and East Asia when they think about children's learning:

• People in America are very largely thinking about résumé virtues.
• People in East Asia are thinking about both résumé *and* eulogy virtues.

Parents and teachers in East Asia intend to guide children toward becoming not only good people but also conscientious pupils who accept some responsibility both for their own learning and for efficient classroom processes.

Three points about how people in East Asia think can now be made:

1. The meaning they give to "good person" includes being a good student, which comprises an expectation that good students study long and hard.
2. They view the learning of personal and social virtues as inseparable from cognitive learning.
3. *To them, studying and learning are inherently virtuous, which is a fundamental difference between their thinking and that of Americans.*

"Teach Books; Cultivate People"

In China, a common saying is *jiāo shū yù rén*. The first two characters translate literally as "teach books." The third character, *yù*, may be translated variously as bring up, raise, rear, nourish, cultivate, or educate. The final character, *rén*, means people. The four characters together capture the fundamental goals of teaching as Chinese people understand them.

In Japan, it's common to talk about a goal of primary teachers as being to guide their pupils toward becoming *ningen*, which basically means "human"—acting appropriately in certain roles as well as in relationships with other humans. Recall the discussion in chapter 2 about the "pedagogy of feeling," and the discussion in chapter 3 about the daily periods of reflection (*hansei*) to evaluate the group and one's contribution to it.

In both China and Japan, developing skills in human relations is a key component of being educated. *Ningen* implies a human with well-honed interpersonal competencies and a sense of empathy, social cohesion, group harmony, and collective responsibility. Insuring that children gain the requisite interpersonal competencies is the process of *yù rén* and is a shared responsibility of teachers and parents.

In the United States, a teacher's responsibility is largely for her pupils' cognitive development. Of course, a teacher necessarily concerns herself with certain aspects of in-school behavior. But within publicly funded systems, teachers must be careful never to overshadow parental prerogatives regarding pupils' deep understanding of morality and ethics.[4]

AN EXCURSION INTO THE HISTORY OF ETHICS

These contrasting educational emphases are often associated in East Asia with Confucius and in the West with Socrates. Confucius and Socrates were near contemporaries.[5] Each was respected in his lifetime as a wise thinker. But neither originated the ethical system with which he has come to be associated. Each is better viewed as a popularizer of ethical trends that had been developing across centuries.

During ancient times, the ways of life in Greece and China were a study in contrasts. It's likely that their dissimilar physical environments led to differences between Greek and Chinese values and ethics.[6]

Because Greece was a land of mountains, rivers, and valleys, large-scale agriculture was impossible. People lived mainly by herding and fishing. They organized themselves into small city-states that retained their independence from each other. It was rare for a powerful ruler to emerge; public decisions usually were made by assemblies of citizens. Also, Greece was a crossroads of trade, which brought new ideas to the public. A Greek could befriend people outside his family, entertain new thoughts, and try to convince others of his ideas. Within this physical and social environment, an emphasis on *individualism* was born.

In China there were mountains, too, but between them were vast stretches of flat, fertile land hospitable to agriculture on a large scale. This required village inhabitants to work together toward a common goal. That, in turn, required organization, planning, and coordination: leadership. Encouraged were values that emphasized getting along well with others, social order within a hierarchy, and fulfilling one's responsibilities to neighbors. Censured were those inhabitants who prioritized their own needs and ideas over the village's welfare or the leader's guidance. These ways of life were the daily experience of millions of villagers across millennia. Within this environment, an emphasis on *collectivism* was born.

When we probe even further into the contrasting patterns of ethical thought emerging from ancient Greece and China, we find an especially deep East-West distinction: *where to seek truth and self-realization*.

Ancient Greeks Valued Introspection[7]

You might have heard the expression "music of the spheres." It was coined by Pythagoras—yes, the guy who devised that theorem about triangles—who lived in Greece during the sixth century BCE. Pythagoras and his followers were fascinated by connections they had discovered among arithmetic, geometry, music, and astronomy—connections they saw as providing insights about all of nature. They were empiricists, but their insights, being mathematical, *required only mental contemplation* and yielded truths that seemed certain and eternal. They experienced this process as one of personal ecstasy, *a revelation from within*. They trusted this knowledge more than that offered by their own five senses.

These ideas were ascendant when, during the fifth century BCE, Plato came of age. A student of Socrates, Plato accepted the then-popular belief that our day-to-day world is a collection of appearances that are inaccurately reported by our five senses. He postulated a parallel world that is "Real," a world of concepts. The most value comes from exploring what's in that eternal, "Real" world because it's infallible and wonderful. Knowledge of it is gained only through mental contemplation.

In other words, *the place to seek truth and self-realization is inside oneself, by means of introspection*. This ancient belief became a strong underlying force in Western thought, giving rise to individualism and eventually to notions of education that prioritized the individual student.

What about Socrates? Although he left no writings, he has always received a great deal of attention because of his habit of asking a series of probing questions of both ordinary people and those with power and authority. In this way, he publicly exposed his interlocutors' ignorance, revealing that their certainties were only unsubstantiated beliefs. After humiliating a number of powerful people, he was sentenced to death. (He cheekily suggested to the court that he ought to be rewarded because of his value to Athens.) Famously, Socrates accepted his sentence—suicide—calmly.[8]

Socrates is important because he criticized people's habit of accepting what others tell them rather than seeking truth within themselves. He and Plato are among the originators of two Western perspectives on learning:

- students can and should do their own exploring and discovering;
- sure knowledge can be gained, and often is, via a flash of intuition.

Ancient Chinese Valued Extrospection

Just like Plato and Socrates on the other side of the planet, Confucius accepted certain ideas that were ascendant in Asia when he came on the scene during the sixth century BCE. Using memorable ways of teaching such as anecdotes and proverbs, Confucius strengthened people's adherence to existing virtues,

adding his own emphases. Three of his areas of focus will aid our grasp of
the East Asian view of learning.

- Confucius consistently emphasized the quality of *rén*, which we earlier
  translated as people, but which can also mean benevolent or humane.[9] He
  held that a good person always acts for the benefit of his group, not for his
  separate advantage. The group he had in mind was primarily one's family,
  and also one's clan, village, and even the wider society. Eventually, "one's
  group" also came to comprise one's colleagues at work and fellow students
  in class.

- A second emphasis of Confucius was the benefits of hierarchy. In all relationships, one member has the senior role and one the junior role. Senior
  and junior each have reciprocal obligations to the other: The junior exhibits
  loyalty and respect toward the senior, in return for which the senior exhibits
  competence as well as parent-like caring and concern toward the junior.
  Consider the teacher-student relationship: the teacher actively guides the
  student toward the cultivation of virtue as well as knowledge, and the student exhibits deep respect for the teacher.

- Finally, Confucius also emphasized the gaining of knowledge through
  study. Gaining knowledge came to mean mastering the classics, that is,
  to be able from memory to flawlessly reproduce and write about certain
  classical texts. Accomplishing this feat required indefatigable, full-time
  study lasting several years, aided by a master's authoritative guidance
  and unsparing criticisms. The miniscule minority who did pass the exams
  became society's administrators and government officials.[10] Confucius was
  convinced that the classics contained deep thinking and valuable lessons
  that would lead people to wisdom, reciprocity, and empathy: "Review the
  old to understand the new; thus one can become a master."[11]

In other words, *the place to seek truth and self-realization is in the wisdom
of the past, and in reciprocally beneficial roles and relationships among
the members of one's groups.* This ancient belief became a strong theme in
East Asian thought, reinforcing existing collectivist tendencies. It also drives
notions of education that make learning from an accomplished master indispensable. These background factors have combined to yield three East Asian
perspectives on learning:

- the knowledge students learn, and the processes by which they go about
  learning it, have already been determined by wise masters;
- certain knowledge is gained only through long, persevering study;

• one's studying should be authoritatively guided and unsparingly critiqued by someone who has previously mastered that knowledge.

THE CULTURE OF LEARNING IN EAST ASIA

"Culture of learning" refers to the fact that, within any society, there are taken-for-granted ways and means of learning that most people tacitly agree on and more or less automatically apply. A culture of learning isn't only about how grown-ups think and act as they prepare children for adult life. It's also about how the children learn how to learn, and about what they come to expect of themselves and others while they're learning.

The Drive to Learn discussed the expectations and values of children in East Asia related to learning. We now turn to the ways in which adults in this region regard learning. Many of these perspectives have been discussed already in the foregoing chapters; here we'll pull them all together. The following five assumptions are central: Learning in primary schools is

• oriented toward transmitting society's accumulated wisdom.
• ultimately about instilling virtue, conceived primarily in terms of group welfare.
• designed to reflect the subject's logic, not to accommodate individual learners' traits.
• viewed as a challenging mental struggle requiring disciplined effort.
• pursued to attain the goal of "equity," not "equality of opportunity."

Transmit Society's Accumulated Wisdom[12]

"Why reinvent the wheel?" expresses prevalent attitudes in East Asia about what's available to be learned. A wheel is a tangible object; it's easy to grasp why it's pointless for each generation of children to reinvent it. In East Asia, this attitude is extended to the many intangible things that children need to learn—and to the step-by-step process for learning each one.

In *To Open Minds*, Howard Gardner gives an example of this attitude in action.[13] One day when he was in China with his wife and small child, Benjamin, they were leaving their hotel. Their room key was attached to a large plastic pendant that discouraged guests from leaving without turning in their key. It could be dropped through a narrow slot, requiring that the pendant be aligned just so. Benjamin always wanted to put the key through the slot, but couldn't align the pendant properly, so he just flailed away while his parents watched patiently.

Invariably, a Chinese person nearby—a stranger or attendant—would come over, grasp the child's hand in his or her own, then gently but firmly guide it to the slot, orient the pendant properly, and deposit the key.

The Chinese helper presumably was thinking something like this: What's the point of trial-and-error flailing? There's only one way to do it. I've mastered it, so I will authoritatively guide this child's hand with the pendant. He will efficiently learn to do it correctly. What a shame his parents aren't training him properly! Oh, well, they're Westerners.

We encountered this assumption about how to learn in chapter 3 during the discussion of kata and "entering through form." It boils down to this: It's essential for learners of all ages and of all subjects—academic, artistic, practical—to *begin by mastering the basics*. The basics are known; how to learn them is known. Both the goal and the path to those basics have been perfected, so why learn them any other way? Trial-and-error methods yield repeated failures and wasted time. Learning the right way and practicing it to mastery rewards success. Self-expression? Creativity? They come later, *after* mastery is attained.

Instill Virtue, Conceived Primarily in Terms of Group Welfare[14]

Earlier chapters emphasized that East Asian education at the preschool and early grade levels is more about instilling virtue than about learning content. Virtue is about molding each child to fit into the group, contribute to its welfare, and self-identify as a group member.

East Asian primary schools have *many* more whole-school and nonacademic events than our schools do. The school year in most parts of East Asia is much longer than ours, yet in primary schools roughly the same amount of time as in the United States is devoted to content learning. The additional time—and there's lots of it—is devoted to a range of activities intended to develop children's aesthetic, physical, moral, and social dimensions, and to do so in ways that shape their altruism, loyalty, cooperation, sensitivity to others, and whole-hearted contribution to group efforts.

Two corollaries of the goal of infusing group-oriented virtue are that there's no interest in encouraging pupils (a) to publicly display their individual distinctiveness, nor (b) to expect that their needs and emotions will be catered to. As quoted at the beginning of chapter 3, a Japanese school official explained that "the goal of education is the reduction of individual differences in children."

Design Learning to Reflect the Subject's Logic, Not the Learners' Traits

As related in *The Aptitude Myth*, in the United States between 1875 and 1925, thinking about how best to educate children in schools underwent a metamorphosis. In 1875, the guiding principle was that children attended school to learn subjects needed in adult life; therefore, the children were expected to adapt to each teacher's organization and delivery of lessons. By 1925, the guiding principle had evolved to be that children attended school to learn in ways that reflected their interests, inborn abilities, and probable life course; so teachers were expected to organize and present their subjects in ways that adapted to the traits and needs of the children, considered as a collection of distinct individuals. The new approach was "child-centered" and "progressive."

Progressive principles gained interest in East Asia during the final decades of the 1900s. In China, a major shift in government policy was announced in 1999: "Education for Quality" proclaimed progressive goals including "fostering creativity and practical skills." Changes in actual classroom teaching were slow to spread, however.[15] One reason is that the operating principle of primary school teachers in East Asia has long been that the internal logic of the content they are teaching is the principal driver of how they organize their lessons. They pay little or no attention to factors such as each pupil's personality, interests, creativity, need to be motivated, antipathy to homework, or "learning style."[16]

But there's a big exception: As we'll see in chapter 5, teachers intensely concern themselves with the most effective ways to present lesson content so that *all* pupils in their class will be able to benefit to some extent.

View Learning as a Challenging Mental Struggle[17]

A consequential contrast between how learning is regarded in the United States and East Asia is that while we do our best to make learning engaging and fun, people in East Asia assume that learning involves a struggle that cannot be won without resolve, discipline, and diligent effort.

Is there no satisfaction involved? On the contrary, there's much satisfaction in store for nose-to-the-grindstone learners in East Asia. They're doing it not only for themselves but also to enhance the "face" of their extended families. Their family members will feel pleased with their outstanding grades *and* admire the intense effort they're devoting to attainment of that result. Furthermore, they're doing it not primarily for some indefinite future use but to enhance their usefulness *now* to other group members. And when exams finally show them at or near the top of the class, they will justifiably gain self-esteem—although the value of modesty will discourage them from showing it openly.

The assumption in East Asia is that, to a considerable extent, everyone needs to work hard to master academic subjects. True, some learners were born with greater intelligence. For those who are less intelligent, the great equalizer is their own single-minded effort and resolve, not pull-out tutoring[18] at taxpayer expense. (But if the challenge is simply too demanding, there's always those cram schools—at family expense.)

Pursue Equity Goals, Not Equality of Opportunity Goals[19]

Equity: It's accepted in East Asia that most students work hard and that some work harder to compensate for their lesser intelligence. In spite of variations in intelligence, *the role of schools is to provide similar instruction for all students* except the profoundly disabled. This "equity model" rests on the assumption that each student accepts much of the responsibility for his or her learning outcome, attained via differentiated effort. It's expected that all students will finish schooling with more or less similar knowledge gains.

Equality of Opportunity: It's accepted in the United States that some students have greater inborn intelligence, and some have less. Nevertheless, it's believed that learning should never be genuinely hard for any student, which would be discouraging. Rather, students should find lessons engaging and dispensed in easy-to-understand increments. So *the role of a school is to provide instruction that is "differentiated" in response to each student's characteristics.* This "equality of opportunity" model rests on the assumption that teachers accept most of the responsibility for each student's learning outcome. In other words, teachers try to equalize each student's *opportunity* to learn by treating them differently. But they're *not* trying to equalize students' *outcomes*. It's expected that students will finish schooling with varying outcomes because, after all, some have greater intelligence and some have less.

A MIRROR FOR AMERICANS

As we look into the mirror of East Asian schooling, what do we notice about *our* schools and the values *we* apply when thinking about them?

- **What "learning" brings to mind:** The mirror tells us that when people in East Asia think about "learning" or "to learn," what comes to their minds is fundamentally different from what comes to our minds. This fact is the principal theme running throughout *The Drive to Learn*.

    The characteristic pattern of thinking about learning among the peoples of East Asia is not an outcome of their schooling. *It's an outcome of their shared cultural assumptions and beliefs.* It's a constellation of values and norms instilled in the very young, largely by their parents and extended family members. Of course, their teachers not only agree with these values and norms but they also embody and model them and explicitly teach them.

    In my view, what comes into the minds of most students in East Asia when they think about learning—their determination and passion to learn even though they expect grueling mental struggles—is one of the most important factors that gives those students a competitive edge as they begin studying academic subjects, and thereby helps to account for their superior performances on the international tests.

- **Virtue as a component of learning:** Accounts of learning in East Asia are uniform in portraying the teacher's role as that of a mentor and model, a transmitter of "eulogy virtues," *and* that of a content expert laying the foundation for her pupils' coming acquisition of "résumé virtues." This is especially true in the lower grades.

  The difference with the United States is subtle; no one would claim that our teachers are totally ignoring the moral dimensions of their pupils' learning, at least insofar as behavior in class and on school property is concerned. But there *is* a difference. The role of American teachers is strongly oriented toward the cognitive and academic development of their pupils. Moral development is almost entirely a parental concern. Furthermore, after children enter first grade, American parents usually relax their active interest in cognitive development, assuming their children's teachers are mainly responsible for that.[20]

  One could easily imagine that the cognitive/academic emphasis of American educators would lead to superior outcomes for American students on the international comparative tests. It does not.

- **The logic of lesson design:** The mirror reminds us that, at least in our rhetoric and theorizing about classroom teaching, we ceaselessly emphasize how important it is to tailor instruction to pupil-related wishes, needs, traits, and styles.

  For example, I just received an education-focused periodical with an article about how pupils in one school are helping to redesign the curriculum. In discussing how the benefits of this initiative were attained by the pupils, the authors write, "If students feel empowered, and if they experience opportunities *to know what they know and feel what they feel....*" There you have a wonderful example of the Western assumption that the place to seek truth and self-realization is inside oneself, by means of introspection.[21]

  But what isn't clear, at least to me, is what's *really* going on behind the scenes when most primary school teachers design and prepare their lessons. How much are they guided by their subject's logic, and how much by the characteristics of their students? What I *suspect* is that the subject's logic continues to play a crucial role—in spite of our constant rhetoric about student-centered pedagogy.[22]

  In my view, if it *is* true that teachers in East Asia, when designing their lessons, are guided far more by their subjects' logic than are American teachers, then that would be another factor that gives students in East Asia a competitive edge as they study academic subjects, and thereby would help to account for their superior performances on the international tests.

Remember, though, that because students across East Asia tend to be more receptive to classroom learning than students in the United States, the classroom dynamic there is much different from that faced by American teachers.

FURTHER READING

If you'd like more detail about the researchers' findings or simply wish to know what inspired the contents of chapter 4, read these entries in the annotated bibliography at www.amirrorforamericans.info.

- Biggs, John B. (2001), Teaching across cultures.
- Cheng, Kai-ming (1998), Can education values be borrowed?
- Cortazzi, Martin (1998), Learning from Asian lessons.
- Damrow, Amy (2014), Navigating the structures of elementary school in the United States and Japan.
- Frkovich, Ann (2015), Taking it with you: Teacher education and the baggage of cultural dialogue.
- Hu, Guangwei (2002), Potential cultural resistance to pedagogical imports.
- Jin, Lixian, & Martin Cortazzi (2006), Changing practices in Chinese cultures of learning.
- Lewis, Catherine C. (1995), *Educating Hearts and Minds*.
- Li, Jin (2003), The core of Confucian learning.
- Li, Jin (2012), *Cultural Foundations of Learning: East and West*.
- Pratt, Daniel, Mavis Kelly, & Winnie Wong (1999), Chinese conceptions of "effective teaching" in Hong Kong.
- Rohlen, Thomas P., & Gerald K. LeTendre (1998b), Conclusion: Themes in the Japanese culture of learning.
- Sato, Nancy, & Milbrey W. McLaughlin (1992), Context matters: Teaching in Japan and the United States.
- Shimahara, Nobuo K., & Akira Sakai (1995), *Learning to Teach in Two Cultures: Japan and the United States*.
- Stevenson, Harold W., & James W. Stigler (1992), *The Learning Gap*.
- Tang, Deden, & Doug Absalom (1998), Teaching across cultures: Considerations for Western EFL teachers in China.
- Tobin, Joseph, Yeh Hsueh, & Mayumi Karasawa (2009), *Preschool in Three Cultures Revisited*.

Chapter 5

Foundations of East Asian Schooling, Part II

How Classroom Teaching Is Regarded

$$12 - 7 = 5$$

The type of problem about which five Japanese lower grade teachers met multiple times over three weeks to devise, pilot-test, and revise a 15-page lesson plan.[1]

Imagine this: In an elementary school, four first- and second-grade teachers decide to improve the way a subtraction lesson is taught to first graders. Over a three-week period, and joined by a vice principal, they meet numerous times in working sessions lasting one to two hours. They develop a twelve-page lesson plan as well as intensively deliberated handouts and manipulatives[2], and debate the best arrangement of information on the blackboard. Then they revise all of this into a thirteen-page version, which is pilot-tested with one participant's first-grade class, while the other four observe and take notes. Another revision follows, then a second pilot session with another class—which was observed by every teacher in the school. Final revisions occur, resulting in a fifteen-page plan. The closing activity is a two-hour all-faculty meeting during which the fine points of this improved subtraction lesson are discussed.[3]

Does that sound like a realistic American scenario?

This scenario occurred at Tsuta Elementary School, a public school near Hiroshima. There, lesson-improvement practices such as this are common and are known as *jugyo kenkyu* or Lesson Study. Similar efforts are common events throughout Japan; in China and Taiwan the same process is often referred to as "research lesson."[4]

Lesson Study, portrayed by advocates as a professional development activity that's far superior to typical U.S. in-service teacher training, has been spreading beyond East Asia. Thanks to an active Lesson Study movement here in the States, it's easy to find out more about it.[5]

You might be wondering how Tsuta's *entire faculty* was able to observe a fifty-five-minute pilot session. Were substitutes looking after all those teacher-free classrooms? No. All other students were left alone with assignments to complete, monitored by the student leader of each classroom.[6]

THE EAST ASIAN CULTURE OF TEACHING

For Tsuta Elementary's teachers to willingly persist through the time- and energy-consuming Lesson Study process, they needed certain internal qualities. Expertise in the fine points of mathematical reasoning informed their quest to help their pupils more readily grasp subtraction. Collegiality and professionalism supplied their resolve to join colleagues in reflection (*hansei*) and make continuous improvements (*kaizen*) to their craft.

They also needed an external environment that supported Lesson Study. At Tsuta Elementary and throughout Japan, detailed multipage lesson plans are the norm, and the teaching of pilot lessons that colleagues observe and later critique is common. On most school days, teachers have two to three hours with no classroom responsibilities. Last but not least, there's a room in every school that's set aside for teachers and readily enables pairs or small groups to collaborate.

In other words, Tsuta Elementary School was immersed in a *culture of teaching* unlike that prevailing across the United States.

"Culture of teaching" means that there's a collection of expectations, norms, and values about *what teachers do* that is shared by educational authorities, school administrators, parents and other community members, the teachers themselves—and even by the children.

Five analogies will help us grasp the East Asian culture of teaching:

- The analogy of the composer and the performer
- The analogy of the virtuoso performer
- The analogy of the academic expert
- The analogy of the pastor
- The analogy of the athletic coach.

The Analogy of the Composer and the Performer[7]

This first analogy calls attention to a significant way in which teaching in East Asia is *unlike* teaching here in the United States.

When we think about people who make their living making music, a distinction that comes readily to mind is that some *compose* music, and some *perform* music. Yes, some do both, but more typical is a performer who offers his or her interpretation of someone else's composition.

This way of explaining how work is divided up in the music world is a good analogy for how teaching is regarded in East Asia. There, everyone agrees that the work of a classroom teacher is to teach, period. It's *not* expected that individual teachers will also create their own curriculum, sequence of topics, and overall emphases. Those essentials—but *not* lesson plans—are provided by each nation's ministry of education.

Researchers who looked into the East Asian mirror while thinking about American teaching realized that, here in the United States, it's expected that good primary school teachers will be creative or innovative. They should both *compose* (develop) lessons and *perform* (deliver) them. All the better if they come up with something unusual and fun that really wows the kids.

The double expectation of American teachers—compose *and* perform—is amplified by another factor: the typical American teacher works largely in isolation, rarely collaborating with fellow teachers in any sustained way to improve lesson plans.[8] (This is exactly what one would expect in an individualistic culture.)

Teachers in East Asia expect to collaborate and share with colleagues, especially with those who (a) teach the same grade and/or (b) have far more teaching experience. An example of an extensive collaborative project began this chapter. But teachers also share ideas and experience on a daily basis. (This is exactly what one would expect in a group-oriented culture.)

Here's where architecture gets involved. In at least one respect, East Asian school architecture diverges from ours: School floor plans include one large faculty room with no partitions where every teacher has his or her desk. Adjacent desks are assigned to teachers of the same grade, which greatly facilitates day-to-day sharing of lesson plans and more.

The Analogy of the Virtuoso Performer[9]

One anthropologist who studied teachers in East Asia found that "performer" didn't capture what she came to appreciate about the teachers she was observing. Instead, she compared them with *virtuoso* performers.

> The class becomes an audience. Involved is much of the dynamic of actor, stage, and audience. The excellent teacher is one who performs for the class as a whole and is able to reach the whole group. The virtuoso impresses and

affects the audience. The virtuoso certainly interprets and responds to the feel of the audience, yet the chief activity—teaching—does not alter for individual members in the auditorium.

The virtuoso teacher is one who has so mastered the technical knowledge of the text that she or he is able to transcend it, adding a piece of one's own self, one's own interpretation, in organizing the presentation, communicating it, and rendering it understandable. As with musicians whom I interviewed, true virtuosity involves not simply "technical wizardry" but also "heart."[10]

A veteran teacher put it this way: "Teaching has a sweet flavor. The good teacher, like the virtuoso musician, is more than an exceptionally competent machine; *there is an affective requirement, the need for heart,* for appreciation of the 'sweet flavor.'"[11]

An American graduate student who visited schools in Beijing observed Lesson Study classes being taught at two elementary schools. In her blog, she "wonders whether or not the lesson had been pre-rehearsed by the teacher and her students."[12] Here's my answer: Virtuoso performers of every description rehearse, at least in their minds. But it's inconceivable that the students in the observed classroom had also been put through a rehearsal session.

The Analogy of the Academic Expert[13]

The notion of a virtuoso performance by any professional implies that he or she has *thoroughly mastered* his or her craft or field. In East Asia, classroom teachers are expected to have mastered their field, to be academic experts. A Chinese proverb notes that, "To give a student a cup of water, the teacher should have a bucket of water."[14]

Having worked tirelessly to become an authority in his or her field, an academic master is well equipped to guide the novice learners who follow. In East Asia, such guidance includes direct, unsparing critiques of the learner's bumbling attempts, which are considered neither by learners nor masters to undermine self-esteem. Pride in accomplishment is one's reward for mastery after intense study.[15]

An important goal for teachers is to present the lesson content so that *all* their pupils will be able to benefit. Yes, this means that the teacher might progress a little slower than the most able children *could* keep up with, and a little faster than the least able ones can grasp without extra effort. But that's OK, because a key objective is for all pupils to progress together. As emphasized previously, the primary years are not a time to highlight children's differences. As a master of her subject, the teacher is well equipped to make these judgments and to patiently assist individuals who are struggling—but not while the lesson is in progress.

Teacher-as-academic-expert isn't merely a well-meaning platitude. Teachers in East Asia are, on average, stronger content experts than their U.S. counterparts. One discouraging comparison was reported by a researcher who interviewed elementary math teachers in China and the United States. The Chinese teachers came from both rural and urban schools; all were graduates of the ninth grade and of teacher training schools. The Americans all had bachelor's degrees; some had master's degrees.

The interviews comprised four questions that probed how each teacher would handle a mathematical concept. The questions increased in difficulty, with the fourth involving complex concepts.[16] The Chinese teachers handled all questions well and some offered multiple solutions. The Americans' responses "revealed disturbing deficiencies."

The researcher then asked the same four questions of ninth graders "at an unremarkable school in Shanghai." She reported that "these Chinese ninth-grade students demonstrated better understanding of the interview problems than did the American teachers."[17]

The Analogy of the Pastor[18]

"Pastor" is derived from a Latin term meaning "shepherd," one who tends to the well-being of a flock of sheep. Many Protestant churches refer to their ministers as "pastors," a term that sidesteps their role as religious leaders and emphasizes their role as benevolent guardians of the moral, physical, and emotional well-being of those under their care.

Similarly, an expected role of a teacher in East Asia is that of a moral guide and mentor, one who not only advises protégés regarding ethical behavior—both when asked and without waiting to be asked—but also models an exemplary life. Chinese university students, asked about a good teacher's qualities, replied that a teacher should "have great virtue"; "be a good model for every student"; and "help me learn more of the world and life so that I can deal with others more successfully."[19]

In addition, a pattern found among the cultures of East Asia is an expectation that teachers have significant responsibility for their pupils' behavior outside the classroom—and even off the school grounds. In fact, if a Japanese child gets up to mischief in the community, witnesses often report it to the school instead of to the child's parents.[20]

In Japan, outside-the-classroom guidance extends all the way to how pupils will spend their vacation. Pre-vacation plans include times of day to arise, study, practice a sport, retire, and so forth. The teacher assists each child in devising a goal-driven schedule; for example, swim 100 meters, upgrade math skills, stop fighting with brother. When the holiday ends, the teacher expects a point-by-point progress report.[21]

The pastor analogy, together with that of the academic expert, is an element in an archetypal East Asian relationship pattern (introduced in chapter 4) known as "senior-junior": in virtually all relationships, both parties are conscious of who is "senior" and who is "junior." Examples include ruler-subject, parent-child, and older sibling-younger sibling. The ideal is *not* for the senior to boss around the junior. Quite the opposite: without waiting to be asked, seniors caringly mentor and advise their juniors regarding their skills, attitudes, values, behavior, relationships, and overall personal development.[22]

The Analogy of the Athletic Coach[23]

Those who base their views of teachers in East Asia solely on observations of secondary or university classrooms often brand the teachers as formal and distant. What they don't observe, or only fleetingly observe, are teacher-student interactions outside the classroom.

When lessons are not in progress, the expectation in East Asia is for teacher-student relationships of two types: pastor-parishioner and coach-athlete. A teacher resembles a coach in that the coach

- has a warm and largely informal relationship with the athlete, one that often encompasses non-sport aspects of the athlete's life;
- maintains high expectations for the athlete's performance;
- instructs the athlete *what to do* (e.g., practice drills), and *how to do it* (e.g., techniques), in pursuit of consistently high performance;
- models and trains the athlete in basic skills and winning techniques;
- advises the athlete about ways of supporting continuous performance improvement (e.g., get more sleep, eat a well-balanced diet);
- disciplines the athlete who fails to follow his or her instructions;
- directly criticizes the athlete for poor techniques or insufficient effort, showing little or no concern for the athlete's self-esteem; and
- regards the athlete's success or failure as his or her own.

TEACHERS' "SENIOR" ROLES:
THEIR INCLINATION[24]

Most teachers in East Asia feel positively inclined to exercise near-parental nurturing, directiveness, and protection toward the youth for whom they're responsible. For one thing, the tradition of "senior-junior" relationships runs deep; it has been a key emphasis since the time of Confucius. For another, the teachers themselves had been "juniors" for at least the first twenty years of their lives. We can imagine that, looking back, many feel deep gratitude toward the "seniors" who mentored them with mind and heart. And all of this occurs in the day-to-day context of a collectivist culture in which people expect and value overtly hierarchical relationships.

In the United States, the egalitarian values of our highly individualist culture lead us to be wary of hierarchies, to attenuate any authority that we have over others, and to try to minimize others' authority over ourselves. It's not that we deny the legitimacy of authority, but that we are uncomfortable giving and receiving it. Teachers in the United States hesitate to assume the role of content expert, portraying themselves instead as fellow learners. They assume that their exercising of authority might damage students' self-esteem, stifle their creativity, or detract from classroom engagement and enjoyment. Across East Asia, a teacher with such attitudes is regarded with skepticism, or worse.

For example, one author has written of her time teaching English to Chinese teachers from rural schools. She and other American teachers were steeped in progressive methods: they portrayed themselves as "well-read colleagues," strove to bring music and fun into their lessons, and refused to correct students' errors in spoken English to "maintain the integrity of their relationships with their (adult) students." However, not correcting students' errors turned out to be interpreted by their students as either lazy or

a clear indication that a foreign teacher is not well-trained or experienced. A teacher is perceived as the ultimate authority on the standard of correctness and, as such, must wield her power. This seems to resonate with the course evaluations submitted by the students, who had tremendous praise for teachers who constantly corrected them and worked exclusively for oral language mastery.[25]

Because American teachers tend to feel uncomfortable with strongly exercising a "senior" role, they forfeit receiving deep respect from their students. They often substitute a need to be liked, which they encourage by behaving in a friendly, egalitarian manner. (Looking back to my own years as a teacher, I see this in myself.) Affection is often positive in human relations, but a need to be liked can undermine a teacher's determination to exercise a mentoring role that would have long-term benefits for her pupils. For teachers in East Asia, responsibly exercising their "senior" role is what's important. Being respected is desirable; being liked isn't a concern.

TEACHERS' "SENIOR" ROLES:
THEIR OPPORTUNITIES

Unlike most of their U.S. peers, primary school teachers in East Asia have many routine opportunities to nurture close relationships with pupils because they're more intensively involved with them in the classroom *and* more extensively involved with them nonacademically.

Intensive Involvement with Pupils in the Classroom

In terms of teachers' classroom involvement with their pupils, two examples stand out: (a) Every day, pupils and teachers work together to clean their classrooms and other sections of the school. (b) Every day they eat lunch together in their classrooms—a practice that's standard across Japan but not in China.[26]

School cleaning: Schools in East Asia employ custodians, but cleaning the school isn't a big part of their jobs. That work is done by the pupils and teachers. *Every day* during the afternoon, fifteen to twenty minutes are set aside for cleaning the classroom, the corridors, and other areas.[27] Every pupil is actively involved. One researcher reprinted classroom cleaning instructions from a teachers' manual: Open the windows, push everything to one side of the room, sweep and wipe the empty floors, repeat for the other side of the room, return all items of equipment to their original places, wipe desks and shelves, empty the trash . . . Oh, and there's this footnote: "The rags should be dry. After cleaning time, they should be rinsed, tightly wrung, and hung on one's desk."[28] Another researcher observed blackboard washing, mat- and rug-shaking, and pupils' "turning the mopping chore into relay races or other chasing, raucous games." "Whether areas are truly cleaner or not," she wrote, "daily experience in the process is as important as the end result."[29]

When a private school serving affluent families decided to abolish children's cleaning, it was soon resumed. The school's seventieth anniversary memorial book, reporting the revival of "educational cleaning," offered this rationale:

> It is necessary for the children to experience that when everybody cooperates and works hard, the classroom becomes very clean and it is easier to study. Repeating such experiences, the children will learn the value of labor, and will spontaneously want to cooperate on their own accord.[30]

Lunchtime in Japan: As related in chapter 1, one anthropologist found that the "Lunch" portion of a Tokyo school's manual was *seven times longer* than the same portion of a New Jersey school's manual. Lunch in Japan is a daily opportunity to inculcate group-oriented social skills because lunch is eaten by all pupils and their teacher in their own classroom, *and is fetched and served by the pupils.* One book I've relied on has a cover photo of four charming children wearing chef hats, standing behind pots of hot food, dishing out portions cafeteria-style to their classmates.[31]

Lunch duty is performed by students in their designated groups (*han*), a duty that rotates weekly. They don the required white hats and white shirts, fetch the lunch carts, serve lunch, and clean up afterward, returning the carts to the appropriate area. Students in each *han* clustered their desks together, covered their desks with luncheon placemats, and had their napkins handy. They sat chatting, laughing, or teasing until the lunch *tōban* called their *han* to line up to receive their meal. At one school, no one started eating until everyone was seated. The *tōban* led grace by bowing and saying, "*Itadakimasu*" ["I humbly receive this"], and fellow students responded in turn.[32]

YouTube videos: For a look at school cleaning, search YouTube for "Japanese Students Clean Classrooms to Learn Life Skills" (duration 1:55). For a look at school lunch, search for "Elementary School Life in Japan—School Meals" (duration 3:33).[33]

Extensive Involvement with Pupils Nonacademically

The school year in most of East Asia is significantly longer than it is here in the United States. But the hours the children spend receiving academic instruction is almost the same as here. So there's plenty of time left for nonacademic in-school activities.[34]

Activities and services for pupils: Like their American peers, pupils across most of East Asia are provided with nonacademic opportunities such as playing and singing music, creating art, participating in physical education and clubs, as well as with supportive services. But there's a big contrast in the way such opportunities and services are delivered.

One researcher listed side by side the roles of all staff members at one elementary school in New Jersey and another in Japan. In the New Jersey school, thirty-three roles included teachers of art, math, music, health/PE, home economics, special education, technology skills, compensatory math, and English as a second language; *plus* non-teaching roles such as nurse, librarian, psychologist, social worker, speech therapist, guidance counselor, learning consultant, and gifted-education coordinator. Also, there were aides and secretaries for seven school functions such as the cafeteria.

The Japanese elementary school had a grand total of *eight* roles: principal, vice principal, nurse, secretary, custodian, school doctor/pharmacist, cafeteria worker, and teacher.[35] So except for health and cafeteria services, the Japanese pupils relied on their classroom teachers for just about everything. "The omnipresence of the classroom teacher," wrote the researcher, "fosters his or her efforts to develop the 'whole child.'"[36] In fact, one role for the teachers was to provide *seikatsu shidō*, or life guidance, with respect to the pupils' goals *and* to their health, safety, self-discipline, and personal hygiene—in general, the habits and skills necessary for their daily lives.[37] Figure 5.1 depicts the difference between the United States and Japan.

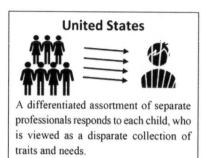

United States	**East Asia**
A differentiated assortment of separate professionals responds to each child, who is viewed as a disparate collection of traits and needs.	One professional (the teacher) responds to all, or nearly all, of each individual child's traits and needs.

Figure by Cornelius N. Grove

Figure 5.1

All-School and grade-level events: A second key distinction between American and East Asian primary schools is that the latter have vastly more all-school and grade-level events than is common here in the United States.

Table 5.1 is a list of the events that occurred during one school year at a Japanese elementary school, excluding "safety/emergency drills," "dental exams," "swimming instruction," and similar activities.

Table 5.1   Events that occurred at a Japanese elementary school during one school year

1. Open school ceremony	16. Art appreciation day
2. Entrance ceremony	17. Music appreciation (fifth grade)
3. Parent observation day	18. Whole-school cleaning
4. School picnic	19. Close second trimester ceremony
5. Home visits	20. Open third trimester ceremony
6. Outdoor classroom (sixth grade)	21. Calligraphy exhibition
7. Camping trip (fifth grade)	22. Parent observation day
8. Close first trimester ceremony	23. New parent (first grade) meeting
9. District swim meet (sixth grade)	24. Social studies field trip
10. Open second trimester ceremony	25. Clubs presentation day
11. Parent observation day	26. Graduation picnic
12. Sports day	27. Giving thanks ceremony
13. District track meet (sixth grade)	28. Good-bye party
14. Science field trip	29. Close third trimester ceremony
15. Community festival	30. Graduation ceremony

Source: Nancy E. Sato (2004). *Inside Japanese Classrooms.* Based loosely on Appendix A, pp. 265–266.

In Japan, such events are meticulously planned so that nothing is left to chance and all performers are well-rehearsed. Faculty planning for these events begins *weeks* in advance and involves several permanent committees. The children participate actively in the planning, often collaborating to write their speaking or singing parts.[38] And each event, large and small, has a written statement of purpose that is related to both community-building and character-building.[39]

Every eligible child participates in all events. "Eligible" means, for example, that if it's a fifth-grade event, then *all* fifth graders are included, including any guilty of serious infractions. As noted in chapter 2, the remedy for unsocial behavior is to integrate the fractious child more tightly into the group, not to isolate him.

What we call *extra*curricular activities aren't extra. Rather, they're viewed as indispensable for fostering community-mindedness as well as developing the children's motivation, self-discipline, and productive work habits. It all reopens the question, "What's basic to education?" As one researcher observed, "The lack of terminology for distinguishing 'academic' from 'non-academic' activities speaks volumes about the East Asians' whole-person conception of the basics."[40]

A MIRROR FOR AMERICANS

As we look into the mirror of East Asian schooling, what do we notice about *our* schools and the values *we* apply when thinking about them?

- **The culture of teaching:** The East Asian mirror enables us to become aware of contrasts between the culture of teaching there and here. The most basic difference is this: teachers in East Asia have a significantly wider range of responsibilities than teachers in the United States. They spend much more time than American teachers inside their schools each day, each week, and each year. They take on a wider variety of duties, including sharing in the administration and program-planning aspects of their schools, and they have broader nonacademic responsibilities including for whole-school and whole-grade events as well as for their pupils' whole-child personal development. They even devote parts of their weekends and vacations to activities with pupils (e.g., teaching swimming) and to professional development.[41]

  Let's admit that these expectations are, for many teachers in East Asia, emotionally demanding and physically exhausting.[42] There probably aren't many American teachers who would be interested in duplicating the daily, weekly, and yearly schedules of their peers in East Asia—even for extra pay.

Nevertheless, reflecting on East Asia's culture of teaching draws us to notice that our goals for children's education are much narrower. Or more accurately, "much more focused." Our focus is largely confined—our "whole-child" rhetoric notwithstanding—to cognitive achievement. As I've said before and will say again: one could easily imagine that the cognitive/academic emphasis of American schooling would lead to superior outcomes for American students on the international comparative tests. It does not.

- **Teachers as experts, or not:** We don't need an East Asian mirror to turn our attention to the inadequate subject-matter preparation of American teachers. It's widely discussed. And the contrast isn't just with teachers in East Asia. Amanda Ripley in her book, *The Smartest Kids in the World*, details the preparation of a teacher in Finland:

> Stara had wanted to teach Finnish, so she'd applied to the Finnish department at the University of Jyväskylä, where she had to sit for a Finnish literature exam. Only 20 percent of applicants were accepted. At Jyväskylä, Stara spent the first three years studying Finnish literature, reading intensively and writing multiple twenty-page papers. Other required courses included statistics. In her fourth year (out of six years of study), she began her teacher-training program.[43]

Earlier in this chapter we saw that *ninth graders* at a non-elite school in Shanghai demonstrated better understanding of complex math problems than American math teachers! In my view, the superior subject-matter preparation of teachers in East Asia is a critically important factor that gives students there a competitive edge and helps to account for their superior performances on the international tests.

- **Teachers' involvement with pupils:** Much more so than teachers in the United States, teachers in East Asia have direct and sustained involvement with their pupils, not only in the classroom but also in a broad variety of multiple all-school and all-grade activities. They believe that what we call *extra*curricular activities aren't extra but rather are indispensable for developing the foundations of academic perseverance and growth.

Since the first time that international comparative tests were given, students from various parts of East Asia have bested their American peers every time, without exception. Could it be possible that East Asia's all-encompassing teacher-student involvement is among the explanatory factors?

FURTHER READING

If you'd like more detail about the researchers' findings, or simply wish to know what inspired the contents of chapter 5, read these entries in the annotated bibliography at www.amirrorforamericans.info.

- Cheng, Kai-ming (1998), Can education values be borrowed?
- Cortazzi, Martin, & Lixian Jin (1996), Cultures of learning: Language classrooms in China.
- Cortazzi, Martin, & Lixian Jin (2001), Large classes in China: 'Good' teachers and interaction.
- Fernandez, Clea & Makoto Yoshida (2004), *Lesson Study: A Japanese Approach to Improving Mathematics Teaching and Learning.*
- Frkovich, Ann (2015), Taking it with you: Teacher education and the baggage of cultural dialogue.
- Grove, Cornelius (1984), U.S. schooling through Chinese eyes.
- Ho, Irene T. (2001), Are Chinese teachers authoritarian?
- Kotloff, Lauren J. (1998), ". . . And Tomoko wrote this song for us."
- Li, Jin (2012), *Cultural Foundations of Learning: East and West.*
- Ma, Liping (1999), *Knowing and Teaching Elementary Mathematics: Teachers' Understanding of Fundamental Mathematics in China and the United States.*
- Paine, Lynn W. (1990), The teacher as virtuoso: A Chinese model of teaching.
- Pratt, Daniel D., Mavis Kelly, & Winnie Wong (1998), The social construction of Chinese models of teaching.
- Rohlen, Thomas P., & Gerald K. LeTendre (1998b), Conclusion: Themes in the Japanese culture of learning.
- Sato, Nancy E. (2004), *Inside Japanese Classrooms: The Heart of Education.*
- Sato, Nancy, & Milbrey W. McLaughlin (1992), Context matters: Teaching in Japan and the United States.
- Stevenson, Harold W., & James W. Stigler (1992), *The Learning Gap.*
- Stigler, James W., Clea Fernandez, & Makoto Yoshida (1998), Cultures of mathematics instruction in Japanese and American elementary classrooms.
- Tsuneyoshi, Ryoko (2001), *The Japanese Model of Schooling: Comparisons with the United States.*
- Usui, Hiroshi (1996), Differences in teacher classroom behaviors in the United States and Japan: A field note.

Chapter 6

East Asian Primary Schools, Part I

How Classroom Lessons Are Delivered

> Westerners whom we have accompanied to classrooms in East Asia are shocked by the frequency with which the teacher calls upon students for their opinions or explanation of a problem, then seeks the reaction of other students to what has been suggested.
>
> Researchers Harold Stevenson and Shin-ying Lee[1]

Two years ago, I began gathering and studying well over 100 peer-reviewed publications about East Asian primary school classrooms written by trained social scientists from many nations, each of whom had spent months, even years, in East Asia recording their observations. Based on their findings, what completely astonishes me is how utterly wrong are the usual stereotypes (such as the one alluded to in the quote above) about East Asian classroom learning.

This chapter and the next two will provide you with a feeling for, as well as an understanding of, what pupils really experience as they participate in academic learning in East Asian primary schools.

As noted in the Introduction, the majority of research into classroom inter-action has been carried out in mathematics classrooms, which is why chapter 7 is devoted to mathematics learning. This chapter, the sixth, relies on a dozen excellent accounts of non-math classes.[2]

SETTING THE STAGE FOR WHOLE-CLASS LEARNING

The phrase "whole-class learning" gets some folks perturbed. Most likely, their thinking goes something like this: If all the pupils in a classroom are learning simultaneously, then their teacher must be telling them stuff—in a word, "lecturing," and that's bad. To be learning, pupils must be active, engaged, talking, questioning, discovering—and those things just can't occur when the entire class is under the teacher's direction.

Suppose it were possible for *both* to be true. It is! In most parts of East Asia

- Entire classes are routinely being directed by their teachers, *and*
- The pupils are active, engaged, talking, questioning, and discovering.

When researchers who are closely familiar with East Asian classrooms discuss the most common mode of instruction there, the phrase they often use is "whole-class *interactive* learning." Let's find out why they add "interactive."

It's no accident that this topic wasn't introduced earlier. East Asian teaching *occurs within a cultural context*, which was discussed in chapters 1–5. They set the stage for this chapter and the next two. Let's review the key points from those five preceding chapters:

From chapter 1:

1. Large class sizes in East Asia help youngsters gain the expectation that teachers can't respond to all of their personal issues. A child's unique needs and concerns are of less importance than the well-being and social development of *all* children in the classroom group.
2. Studying how best to learn their language's written characters familiarizes children with ways of mastering a demanding mental (and muscle memory) task with rigor, discipline, and perseverance, qualities transferrable to other subjects and endeavors.

From chapter 2:

3. Group orientation, with its emphasis on empathy, harmony, and shared objectives, is strongly inculcated in preschool classmates. In Japan, a key educational goal is the reduction of children's individual differences.

From chapter 3:

4. Preschoolers in Japan learn that there's a right way to do something (*kata*) that everyone must master. The established process for learning it needs to be applied by the novice with active guidance and unsparing critiques by someone who already has mastered it.
5. Children are taught how to pay attention, how to interact with the teacher during a lesson, how to coordinate with peers, and how to share responsibility with the teacher for the delivery of efficient, focused learning activities.

From chapter 4:

6. People in East Asia think of "learning" not only in practical terms, but even more so in moral terms. The meaning they give to "good person" includes being a good student, one who studies long and hard to mastery.
7. Teachers use the internal logic of their subject matter as the principal driver of how they organize their lessons; they pay little attention to the unique needs, interests, and abilities of their individual pupils.

From chapter 5:

8. Key characteristics of the East Asian culture of teaching are that teachers are thoroughly grounded in their academic specialties, that much time and thought go into their planning of each day's lesson, and that teachers collaborate on the best ways to teach each lesson.
9. Teachers concern themselves with the most effective way to present lesson content so that *all* pupils in their class will be able to grasp it, with the proviso that the most able pupils will need to tolerate a slow pace, and the least able will need to apply determined effort.
10. A characteristic that applies to the interpersonal features of the cultures of East Asia is the "senior-junior" relationship pattern. It infuses the teacher-pupil relationship so that twin aspects of any teacher's role are relating to pupils as a caring pastor *and* a demanding athletic coach.

With the stage thus set by that integrated collection of assumptions and values, whole-class *interactive* learning emerges more or less organically.

TEACHER, LEARNERS, KNOWLEDGE, AND INTERACTIVITY

Any learning situation comprises three key elements: teacher, learners, and knowledge. The role each plays varies from one culture to another. How is each marshaled in support of whole-class *interactive* learning?

The Role of the Teacher in Whole-Class Interactive Learning

Given the cultural context created by the ten assumptions and values that we've just reviewed, people in East Asia came to believe that the most appropriate classroom role for teachers is one that probably is best characterized as *directive*.

It's significant that the best characterization is not "authoritarian," which implies rigidity, punishment, and emotional coldness. Primary school teachers in East Asia rarely act in an authoritarian manner. Most if not all of their pupils respect them as their pastors and coaches, and as experts who already have mastered the material to be learned. The pupils' cultures have conditioned them to be receptive—attentive—to experts.[3] They see that their teachers are thoroughly prepared to present the contents of lessons. Consequently, acting in an authoritarian manner is rarely necessary for teachers *within the cultural context of East Asia.*

But that same cultural context makes it appropriate for teachers to be "directive" while presenting lessons in the sense that they *take charge of their pupils' learning* in two ways:

- **Process management:** Teachers plan and direct the process by which pupils learn. For example, relative to Americans, Chinese teachers give more "regulatory instructions" before a classroom activity, thus proactively directing pupils' step-by-step learning behavior.[4]

- **Content management:** Teachers in East Asia know their pupils very well, not only as individuals but also in terms of the group's current level of progress with the content to be learned. Through experience and collegial collaboration, teachers know the aspects of a lesson that their pupils are likely to find difficult to grasp. So teachers tweak and refine strategies that will foster their students' understanding. The resulting lesson is a complete and coherent experience; like a story, it has an interconnected beginning, middle, and end.[5]

Finally, teachers in East Asia are grounded not only in mastery of their respective academic fields but also in thorough familiarity with their pupils' textbooks. On these bases, they prepare and present each day's lesson.

Textbooks? We've barely mentioned textbooks so far. Textbooks in East Asia are strikingly different from American ones, both inside and out. We'll discuss their contents and appearance in chapter 8.

The Role of the Pupils in Whole-Class Interactive Learning

Pupils in East Asia begin a lesson expecting activities to occur that are unlike those expected by pupils in the United States. How they expect to behave, and why, is best described by using an analogy (but one that falls short, as we'll soon see):

The religious service analogy.[6] Imagine that you are attending a service at a church or synagogue. The activities of the service follow a pattern devised by, and proclaim teachings written by, wise elders in the past. The service is led by a religious leader who has prepared it carefully, drawing on years of theological study.

Your role is to watch and listen, appreciating (or not) the wisdom of the elders and the demeanor and oratorical skill of the leader. Most assuredly, *your role is never to interrupt.* You silence your phone, suppress your coughs, and don't even think of jumping in with a question about something you didn't "get." The service is set apart for the contemplation of the wisdom of those long-gone elders and the persuasive appeals of the living leader. This time also belongs to your fellow participants, who (like you) presumably have come to gain mental or spiritual benefits. All of you show respect for this special time by remaining mentally engaged—and physically quiet. Consider:

- *The knowledge* that is the focus of a classroom lesson is analogous to the elders' wisdom that's the underlying reason for a religious service.

- *The teacher* is analogous to the religious leader who has conscientiously prepared to deliver not only the elders' wisdom but also the entire experience. Like the religious leader, the teacher expects to deliver the experience *for all participants as a group*, not to use this special time to respond to the needs of individuals.

- *The pupils* are analogous to the participants in a religious service. They anticipate that their minds will follow wherever the leader leads, that their role is to participate amenably when expected to do so (such as reciting or chanting texts in unison), and that they must not interfere with the planned proceedings. Yes, they might have questions, new ideas, or even disagreements. Fine. But it's not appropriate to openly express any of them *now*.

Where this analogy falls short. This analogy allows people to continue imagining that teachers in East Asia "lecture" to pupils who are "passive" listeners. That is false.

Pupils taught through "whole-class interactive learning" aren't just watching and listening. That's not possible because *teachers in East Asia frequently pose questions that arouse curiosity or reveal perplexity*, then call for responses from pupils by name (usually, *not* from volunteers).

Two more things: first, classrooms in East Asia (especially Japan) are often described as having a "buzz." Pupils are expected to confer with each other about the mental challenges coming from their teachers. Second, lessons are *never, ever interrupted* by all-school announcements, lunch-count monitors, or pupils being "pulled out" for special athletic or music practice sessions, or for compensatory instruction. Lessons hold a privileged place in the activities of an East Asian school.[7]

The Role of "the Knowledge" in Whole-Class Interactive Learning

The knowledge refers to whatever is to be learned: for example, mathematics, reading, science, or history, or even something more skill-based such as art, music, or swimming. In this book we are concerned with how children in various parts of East Asia acquire academic knowledge.

American educators refer constantly to the distinctions separating "teacher-centered" and "child-centered" classrooms. Over the years, my experience with these two terms has been exactly like that of three respected researchers who wrote:

> Looking across our interviews with U.S. early childhood educators, we find no instance of "teacher-directed" being used positively or of "child-centered" being used negatively. Indeed, the term "child-centered" functions as a metonym for progressive practice and "teacher-centered" as a metonym for regressive approaches.[8]

What I've noticed is that, while Americans vie with each other to praise child-centeredness and denigrate teacher-directiveness, *the knowledge* gets relatively little sustained attention. So the fundamental reason why children come to school is being overshadowed.

What is the role of the knowledge in American classrooms?

It hasn't been totally forgotten. Rather, our teachers' efforts to impart it have been driven less by the characteristics of the knowledge, more by the characteristics of the pupils plus a set of ideas about what it takes to "engage" pupils' attention.

Whether or not that assessment resonates with you, you now should be able to recognize that the role of "the knowledge" in East Asian primary schools is significantly greater than it is in most American primary schools. This is one of the most important revelations of this book.

A noteworthy finding to emerge from research in this field concerns *interactive time-on-task*. It's a measure of the percentage of the class period during which teacher and all pupils are united in focusing on the "task"—that is, the knowledge—via instruction, explanation, and questioning (but not silent reading or seatwork). Drawing on several studies, a comparison was made between schools in the United States and China. The interactive time-on-task in China was 81 percent of class time; in the United States it was 44 percent.[9]

Let's stop talking in generalizations and percentages. It's time to visit some East Asian classrooms where academic lessons are underway.

DETAILED ACCOUNTS OF LESSONS IN EAST ASIA

Moment-by-moment descriptive accounts of academic lessons in the primary grades are extremely tedious to read. So I've edited for clarity and brevity four accounts that describe lessons in China and in Japan.

Language Lessons for Chinese Third and Fifth Graders

Four researchers compared third- and fifth-grade lessons in India and China in urban, semi-urban, and rural schools. In China, class sizes ranged from thirty to over sixty. One of the rural schools was viewed as an elite boarding school for children of party officials, but another didn't even have a toilet (pupils had to walk into the village).[10] Chinese language lessons were organized around stories such as "Wonderful Stones on Mountain Huang." Here's the researchers' description:

A common structure was for the teachers to (1) review the previous day's lesson briefly, (2) introduce a new topic, (3) ask questions and take the pupils through the text, (4) assign class work, and (5) summarize the lesson.

Each lesson addressed a selection of three to five paragraphs for intensive study. When children were asked to read passages aloud, considerable emphasis was placed on developing skills to evoke appropriate emotion.

Most of the questions posed were open-ended. There was a strong preponderance of higher-level questions such as Why? Anything else? How? Pupils were encouraged to be imaginative, and to use "I feel" and "In my opinion" statements. In one instance, the children were asked to invent descriptive names for rocks. In another, a teacher asked, "You said the sentence reflects the author's imagination. Why do you say that?"

Much use was made of children sharing selected readings in pairs to find answers to questions set by the teacher. One teacher asked for a child to be a "little teacher" to explain something to the others.

Teachers wanted to ensure that the students could express their feelings and defend their ideas. Here's an example from the fifth grade ["P" designates a succession of responding pupils]:

T: What was he thinking about?
P: He wanted to hold the violin; he was praying and longing to own that violin.
T: He was praying and longing for it.

P: The word "knelt" usually indicated people in lower level to people in higher level. However, in the mind of Yangke [a story character], the violin is superior level and more important than his life.

T: The violin is sacred, isn't it. We can see the violin is unattainable and very sacred. He will feel content even if he touches it once.

P: I feel what Yang Jin [another pupil] said is somewhat wrong. Yangke knelt in front of the violin because he was afraid of waking up others. The sound he made when he knelt down was very quiet, but if he walked away, he would be found and be beaten, so he knelt there.[11]

The researchers concluded that "in India, classroom practices were teacher-led and textbook-based; the teachers did most of the talking. In China, the approach was more constructivist and student-directed; *the children were talking more than the teacher*."[12]

A Social Studies Lesson for Japanese Fifth Graders

A researcher in Japan painstakingly observed two fifth-grade teachers in different schools in the Tokyo area. One teacher, in a working-class area, had a class of thirty-seven children; the other, in an affluent area, had a class of thirty-two. After reviewing the two teachers' ways of teaching math, the researcher turns to their handling of social studies lessons:

During social studies, teachers lectured more often than during math but interspersed their lectures with questions. The result was a guided question-answer discussion with the whole group.

Most often, questions were not open-ended; rather, teachers sought specific information. One way to get a sense of everyone's opinion without asking each student individually was to solicit answers, then ask who agreed and who disagreed. Among the disagreers, teachers then solicited more opinions, or gave information and asked further questions to make students rethink or clarify their responses.

Usually, if a student came close to the train of thought the teachers wanted to follow, they praised the answer, rephrased it, and continued providing the intended information. Sometimes their discussion changed in response to a student question or comment that sparked an unplanned idea.

The teachers had interesting ways to make sure pupils understood and to maximize participation. For example, after a pupil answered, the group responded orally whether or not they agreed. The "I disagree" responses brought forth lively reactions or discussions. Sometimes the teachers asked, "Who understands?" and "Who does not understand?" Those who did not understand received attention. Sometimes teachers called on pupils to explain why they supported a particular answer.

If the same pupils kept raising their hands, teachers occasionally admonished others for not contributing. Mr. Ito sometimes tossed out barbs like, "Oh, only the girls know the answer?" Another common method was just to call on someone at random.

Sometimes the teachers selected pupils who they felt had more interesting or correct answers. Sometimes they selected pupils who they felt were not paying attention or did not understand, after which they would help them come to an answer.

Ultimately, the teachers wanted to get as many pupils speaking up as possible. One teacher had a deck of cards with a pupil's name on each; he shuffled the deck and drew cards to solicit responses. In some cases when three or fewer hands were raised, to increase participation teachers would ask pupils to consult in groups before answering.[13]

Lest we forget that teachers' personalities are also a factor in how classrooms are run, here's the researcher's observations about the two teachers she followed: one was "more lively and interactive in eliciting student responses and in allowing for between-student consultation." The other had a style "prompting a more subdued class atmosphere and less between-student interaction."[14]

A Reading Lesson for Chinese Fourth Graders

A research team in China recorded this minute-by-minute account of the first twenty minutes of a reading lesson for fifty fourth graders:

Minutes 1–2: The teacher introduces the topic: to study "There's Only One Earth." She asks several pupils to stand and read a character or word aloud.

Minute 3: The teacher asks a question; several pupils answer when called upon. She gives a follow-up explanation to two answers.

Minutes 4–6: The teacher announces a writing task. She gives some pupils a card on which to write answers and asks others to write in their notebooks. She says, "You all write very well." After a while, she collects some cards and sticks them on the board.

Minute 7: The teacher directs pupils to stop writing and read the cards on the board. She asks a question.

Minute 8: After asking another question, the teacher asks the pupils to engage in a discussion with their classmates. She then asks some who finish discussing, one by one, to write their conclusion on the board.

Minute 9: The teacher follows-up with other questions. She inquires, "Any other answer? Why?" Pupils take turns standing to read their answers from their notebooks. The teacher seeks confirmation from anyone that the answers are correct.

Minute 10: The teacher asks the pupils, individually but simultaneously, to read aloud a short text selection.

Minutes 11–12: The teacher asks the pupils to discuss an issue in groups of four. Paired seatmates turn around in their fixed seats to talk with the pair behind them.

Minutes 13–14: The teacher asks a representative from a few groups to report on their discussion. The teacher intersperses the reports with praise and comments.

Minute 15: The teacher asks the pupils, individually but simultaneously, to read aloud a short text selection.

Minute 16: The teacher asks the pupils to take turns reading aloud to their seatmates.

Minute 17: The teacher asks one pupil to stand and read a passage aloud while everyone listens.

Minute 18: The teacher asks a few questions regarding the text; pupils take turns standing and responding.

Minutes 19–20: The teacher plays recorded music and asks all pupils, in chorus, to read the entire text aloud to the rhythm of the music.[15]

The researchers note that this lesson comprises a structured series of activities. During her planning, the teacher took into account timing, pace, variety of activities, brevity of each activity, and transitions between activities. All processes including transitions are smooth, thanks to the "learner-trained learning" that all children undergo in preschool and first grade. The above lesson was teacher-directed *and* the learners were constantly contributing.[16]

Japanese and American Lesson Teaching Compared

A Japanese developmental psychologist on the faculty of the University of Education in Hokkaido accepted a visiting scholar opportunity at the University of Michigan. While there, he visited several primary schools, then wrote an article discussing the differences he'd found between Japanese and American classroom practices. Following are excerpts from four of his eighteen comparisons.

Lesson Introductions: Introductions by American teachers of new problems or units seemed rather abrupt and brief. It's as if spending time laying out the setting for a problem is a waste of time.

Japanese teachers place high priority on just how the lesson gets started to ensure discussion within the whole class. At times they introduce a topic as if they do not know the answer to the question they've just raised as a way of encouraging the whole class to resolve the challenge together.

Teachers in Japan very carefully organize introductions so that all children can have clear conceptual access to the new materials. They assume that instruction that depends on individual differences in knowledge about the new material will not work well. They often ask the more advanced children to hold their answers for a while.[17]

Discussions among Pupils: Over and over again in the United States, I had the feeling that the teachers were hosts of a quiz show: The teacher asks a question, a pupil answers, and the teacher announces whether the answer is correct or incorrect but doesn't explain one way or the other.

This pattern was salient for me because it contrasted with Japanese teaching in which discussions among students are more prevalent. The teacher's role is more like a coordinator than a judge of students' responses. Indeed, Japanese teachers have coined the word *neriai*—"kneading ideas"—to describe the process occurring among pupils. Emphasized is the importance of sharing beliefs during which each child has many opportunities to elaborate and criticize ideas as well as to receive the same from classmates.

Several instructional techniques have been invented to promote children's participation in, and control of, discussions. For example, a teacher will often refrain from directing who will speak next. Instead, the class might adopt a convention that when a pupil has finished speaking, s/he designates the next speaker.[18]

Number of Topics Covered: It always seemed to me that instruction in the U.S. did not focus and dwell on a major theme or problem. Teachers seemed to prefer moving from one topic to another in quick succession. I sometimes had difficulty keeping up with the shifts. I'm aware of the emphasis on quickness in Americans' lifestyle; for example, learning to speed read. In Japan, this type of skill training is not so popular.

Japanese language teachers emphasize *kodawari*, "obsession." They might make children focus on a single word or phrase, continuously coming back to subtle differences, and encouraging pupils to activate their images of, and empathy with, the writer and characters.[19]

Using the Chalkboard: Teachers in the U.S. schools I visited did not seem to consciously organize their writing on the chalkboard in a way that would help promote communication with students.

In Japan, the chalkboard is a primary medium of communication. Teachers are always aware of clarity, size, shape as well as saliency of the items placed there. On the top of the board, they use colored chalk and careful underlining to indicate emphases, and they embellish this by using framing, larger letters, and the edge as well as the point of the chalk.[20]

A MIRROR FOR AMERICANS

As we look into the mirror of East Asian schooling, what do we notice about *our* schools and the values *we* apply when thinking about them?

- **How lessons are delivered:** The East Asian mirror reveals an approach to teaching that some might view as an oxymoron, but that's standard practice in East Asia: *whole-class interactive learning*. It consists of (a) the teacher, who directs all the pupils simultaneously during most or all of the period; (b) the pupils, who frequently contribute substantive inputs for the lesson; and (c) the knowledge to be learned, which consistently is the focus of everyone's attention.

Let's notice, too, what usually is *not* a feature of these lessons: stratagems used by the teacher to engage pupils' interest but are not directly related to the knowledge. Researchers' accounts virtually never describe any teacher-devised activity that's "entertaining" or "motivating" for the pupils, cloaking its real objective: getting pupils to learn as a by-product of participation. A good example of such an activity is "spelling baseball," played in some U.S. English classes to encourage pupils' engagement in learning to spell.[21]

Two experienced researchers, whose careers were defined largely by their comparisons of East Asian and U.S. classroom learning, concluded that *the whole-class approach gives the largest number of children the greatest amount of their teacher's time.*[22]

In my view, the knowledge-centered manner in which primary school lessons are delivered is a crucially important factor that gives students across East Asia a competitive edge and helps to account for their superior performances on the international tests. We will return to this subject in chapter 9, the final chapter of this book.

FURTHER READING

If you'd like more detail about the researchers' findings, or simply wish to know what inspired the contents of chapter 6, read these entries in the annotated bibliography at www.amirrorforamericans.info.

- Cortazzi, Martin, & Lixian Jin (1996), Cultures of learning: Language classrooms in China.
- Cortazzi, Martin, & Lixian Jin (2001), Large classes in China: 'Good' teachers and interaction.
- Hess, Robert D., & Hiroshi Azuma (1991), Cultural support for schooling: Contrasts between Japan and the United States.
- Ho, Irene T. (2001), Are Chinese teachers authoritarian?
- Jin, Lixian & Martin Cortazzi (2006), Changing practices in Chinese cultures of learning.
- Kotloff, Lauren J. (1998), ". . . And Tomoko wrote this song for us."

- Lan, Xuezhao, et al. (2009), Keeping their attention: Classroom practices associated with behavioral engagement.
- Pratt, Daniel D., Mavis Kelly, & Winnie Wong (1998), The social construction of Chinese models of teaching.
- Rao, Nirmala, et al. (2013b), The classroom context: Teaching and learning language.
- Sato, Nancy E. (2004), *Inside Japanese Classrooms: The Heart of Education.*
- Stevenson, Harold W., & James W. Stigler (1992), *The Learning Gap.*
- Stevenson, Harold W., & Shin-ying Lee (1997), The East Asian version of whole-class teaching.
- Stigler, James W., & James Hiebert (1999), *The Teaching Gap.*
- Teddlie, Charles & Shujie Liu (2008), Examining teacher effectiveness within differentially effective primary schools in the People's Republic of China.
- Tsuchida, Ineko, & Catherine C. Lewis (1998), Responsibility and learning: Some preliminary hypotheses about Japanese elementary classrooms.
- Tsuneyoshi, Ryoko (2001), *The Japanese Model of Schooling: Comparisons with the United States.*
- Usui, Hiroshi (1996), Differences in teacher classroom behaviors in the United States and Japan: A field note.
- Winner, Ellen (1989), How can Chinese children draw so well?

Chapter 7

East Asian Primary Schools, Part II
How Mathematics Lessons Are Delivered

American students, watching a videotape of a Japanese mathematics lesson, inevitably react to the pace: They perceive an unbearable slowness. The pace is slow, but the outcome is impressive.

Researchers Harold Stevenson and James Stigler[1]

Sally is having a party. The first time the doorbell rings, one guest enters. The second time the doorbell rings, three guests enter. The third time the doorbell rings, five guests enter. Each time the doorbell rings, the number of guests entering is two larger than entered on the previous ring. *How many guests will enter on the fifth ring?*

The "doorbell problem" was given by researchers to pupils in the United States and China[2] to compare how they think about math and how they go about solving problems. There are two ways of approaching this problem: "concrete" and "abstract/symbolic."

Concrete: Notice that after one guest enters on the first ring, each ring brings two more guests. So add a 1 and a series of 2s to find the answer. How many guests enter on ring 5? That would be 1+2+2+2+2 = 9.

When there are only a few rings, this "concrete" or "counting" solution process works well. But as the number of rings increases—How many guests on ring 55?—more and more children and adults need to make drawings or notes, which can yield the correct answer but (a) is labor intensive and (b) fails to use a strategy that efficiently solves similar but larger problems.

Abstract/Symbolic: Notice that the number of guests who enter on a given ring equals twice the ring number, minus one (because on the first ring, one guest entered instead of two). To use symbols, we'll say that g is the number of guests and n is the ring number. So we can state that $g = 2n - 1$,

79

an "abstract" formula that works with small *and large* problems. How many guests enter on ring 5? That would be $g = (2 \times 5) - 1$; $g = 10 - 1$; $g = 9$. How many on ring 55? Without being labor intensive, that would be $g = (2 \times 55) - 1$; $g = 110 - 1$; $g = 109$.

On one of the rings at Sally's party, 99 guests enter. Which ring?

Answering via the concrete method is very labor intensive. But if we use the formula we just devised, we can quickly determine the answer: $99 = 2n - 1$; adding 1 on both sides of the equal sign yields $99 + 1 = 2n$; $100 = 2n$; $50 = n$.

Using this 99-guests problem, researchers found a difference between Chinese and American pupils that other studies also found.[3] As shown in Table 7.1, Chinese pupils are more likely to approach a challenging problem on a conceptual level—that is, to apply an abstract/symbolic strategy—which amplifies their capacity both to efficiently attain the correct answer and to recognize that more than one strategy can attain the correct answer.

Table 7.1   Solution Strategies: Doorbell Problem with Ninety-Nine Guests[4]

Solution strategy	CHINESE PUPILS		AMERICAN PUPILS	
	Percent trying to apply this strategy	Of those who tried, percent succeeding	Percent trying to apply this strategy	Of those who tried, percent succeeding
Concrete Counting that applies only to *this* problem, not others	29%	37%	75%	46%
Abstract Developing a formula that applies to similar problems	65%	98%	11%	60%

Source: Jinfa Cai & Victor Cifarelli (2004). Thinking mathematically by Chinese learners: A cross-national perspective. *How Chinese Learn Mathematics: Perspectives from Insiders*. Based on portions of Table 4, p. 88.

A DETAILED ACCOUNT OF A
MATH LESSON IN TAIWAN

One study provided this account of a fifth-grade teacher in Taiwan who was presenting a geometry lesson to a large class.

The teacher drew attention to an unusually shaped figure she had neatly drawn on a small blackboard before the class began. She asked how they might go about finding the area of a shaded region, saying, "I don't want you to tell me what the actual area is, just tell me the approach you would use to solve the problem. Think of as many different ways as you can to determine the area shaded with yellow chalk."

She allowed the pupils several minutes to work in small groups and then called on a child from each group to describe the group's solution. Each child came to the front of the room to make his or her statement while pointing to the figure. After each description, many of which were quite complex, the teacher asked members of the other groups whether the procedure described could yield a correct answer.

After several different procedures had been suggested and evaluated by the class, the teacher moved on to a second figure and repeated the entire sequence of steps. Neither teacher nor pupils attained a solution to either problem until all of the alternatives had been discussed.

The lesson ended with the teacher's affirming the importance of seeking multiple solutions—to life's problems as well as to math problems.[5]

This lesson wasn't only described in writing. It was also videotaped and was included in a video about East Asian primary schools produced by the University of Michigan during the 1980s. The video was made to answer queries such as "What's distinctive about teaching styles in China and Japan?"[6]

To watch this video, go to YouTube and search for "University of Michigan, The Polished Stones." (Ignore videos about polishing stones.) The entire video is thirty-five minutes long; the lesson mentioned here begins at the twelve-minute mark. Notice the size of the class.

GENERAL FEATURES OF EAST ASIAN MATH LESSONS

Students in East Asia aren't superior only in math. Yet, how they learn math has drawn a disproportionate amount of interest. Here's why:

The technical details of math never vary, and the way in which math is written (using numbers and symbols such as = and $\sqrt{}$) is nearly universal. But *how* math is taught varies from place to place. So math affords a unique opportunity for researchers to compare "the how" of teaching across cultures, one that avoids the complications resulting from variations in the contents of "the what" being taught. Consider the following problem.

What is the area of a triangle with such-and-such dimensions? The answer is identical everywhere, as are efficient methods of finding it. This is true of no other subject expect perhaps physics or chemistry.

The effort to understand "the how" of East Asian math teaching has yielded insights of two types: *general features* and *specific strategies*. We'll begin with these general features:

- The stance of the teacher vis-à-vis the pupils
- The handling of pupils' errors in reasoning
- The lesson's pace and degree of focus
- The nature of classroom verbal interactions.

The Stance of the Teacher vis-à-vis the Pupils[7]

"Stance" refers to the attitude, mental and emotional, that the teacher takes toward the youngsters arrayed before him or her—*and* toward the knowledge those youngsters are learning.

In chapter 6 we noted that teachers in East Asia are "directive" but rarely "authoritarian." For example, during math lessons, the teacher is not the one who authoritatively decides whether a pupil's solution or answer is correct. That's unlike the usual practice here in the United States, where teachers usually *are* the arbiters of correct and incorrect: when a pupil replies to a question, it's virtually always the teacher who pronounces the answer right or wrong.

Recall the description (and video) of that fifth-grade geometry lesson. After each group's procedure for finding the area was proposed, the teacher *asked members of the other groups* whether that procedure could yield a correct answer. East Asian teachers leave the analysis of correct or incorrect to their pupils (but ensure they get it right!).

With this stance in mind, let's revisit one of the analogies drawn in chapter 5: the teacher as a virtuoso performer. Noting how often and how meaningfully pupils contribute to math lessons, two researchers suggested replacing the virtuoso analogy with *orchestra conductor*.[8]

They could have proposed *facilitator* or *coordinator*, but they stayed with the musical theme. Unfortunately, orchestra conductor doesn't work; conductors rehearse their orchestras until all the players are highly familiar with the conductor's vision for the musical piece to be performed. Teachers and pupils *never* rehearse classroom lessons, not even lessons that will be publicly piloted under the Lesson Study process.

The Handling of Pupils' Errors in Reasoning[9]

Errors in reasoning are inevitable in primary school math classes. How are pupils' incorrect ideas dealt with by teachers in East Asia?

This question relates to an East-West cultural difference that was discussed in chapter 3 of *the Drive to Learn*: how people react to success and failure. Failure in the United States tends to be embarrassing, so people try to minimize or ignore it. Teachers assume that a pupil's faulty reasoning or incorrect answer will demotivate him, so they say nothing and move on to other pupils until they get the right answer.

Things could hardly be more different in East Asia. There, mistakes suggest a path for exploration. The teacher, without pronouncing an answer wrong, will ask the pupil how it was mathematically derived. The pupil explains. The other pupils listen; when asked, they chime in with one or more alternative derivations. Class discussion eventually yields the correct answer.

Here's the point: in East Asia, exploration of the reasoning that led to each error is an important contributor to pupils' conceptual grasp of whatever they're learning. Teachers' *directive facilitation* of the pupils' learning process is enhanced by analyses (by teacher and/or pupils) of the step-by-step reasoning that led to an incorrect answer.

There's no evidence that pupils whose errors are publicly dissected feel embarrassed. The spirit that prevails isn't "gotcha!" Rather, the spirit is that we're all collaboratively involved in analyzing reasoning methods. So instead of being an embarrassment, failure usually is viewed as providing new guide-posts for finding effective ways to do something.[10] For pupils, it's all rather matter-of-fact:

Interviewer: What would happen if you answered incorrectly?
Student: Incorrectly? Just sit down and the teacher would ask another student to answer.
Interviewer: How do you feel then?
Student: Nothing. Wrong means wrong. This time wrong, next time it will not be wrong anymore.[11]

The Lesson's Pace and Degree of Focus[12]

Some believe that the explanation for the academic superiority of students from East Asia is that, year after year, their lessons progress through the material faster than American lessons, enabling older students to know more.

Researchers discovered that the reverse is true. Asian classes proceed at a slower pace, a fact easily observed in math classrooms.

In one study, the number of topics covered during math lessons in a number of first-grade classes was counted. The average number of topics during the lessons in the United States was 4.17; the average in Taiwan was 3.55; the average in Japan was 2.35.[13]

The learning objectives of all the lessons were single-digit and multidigit operations, and place value: three topics. During the U.S. lessons, eight *other* topics were also discussed, including time, money, calendar, and (the second most-discussed topic) fractions. During lessons in Taiwan, three other topics were discussed. During the Japanese lessons, only two other topics were discussed.

So the American pupils are learning more math, right? Wrong. More topics are being *mentioned* in each class, but the pupils are having fewer opportunities to make progress toward mastering the handful of topics that are that lesson's objectives.

Shorthand ways of describing American and Japanese teaching methods have been proposed. Americans believe a teacher should subdivide a lesson into small steps so that most students will quickly grasp each one, after which the teacher moves to the next one. This strategy has been called *quick and snappy*. In Japan, pupils are expected to linger over the issues introduced by the lesson. Teachers pose thought-provoking questions and expect inquiring pupil-to-pupil exchanges that lead to long-answer resolutions. This strategy has been termed *sticky probing*.[14]

The Nature of Classroom Verbal Interactions[15]

Pupils in East Asian primary schools talk more during math classes than Americans. For example, a research team devised a way to measure the quantity of pupils' classroom talk. During lessons on triangles and fractions, Japanese pupils publicly spoke approximately twice as much as their American peers. Furthermore, the word count of Japanese pupils' statements was far greater than the length of the Americans' statements. All of this talking slows the pace but strengthens the learning.

But what are they talking *about*? Another research team looked at fourth- and fifth-grade math lessons in China and the United States, comparing the nature of lengthy classroom discussions. Here's what they found:

The Chinese teachers' questions usually prompted their pupils to explain their procedures ("How did you get that answer?"), to state their mathematical reasoning ("Why was that procedure appropriate?"), or to cite an applicable rule ("What's the rule governing that?"). They also used discussions to promote pupils' awareness of the underlying rules. The outcome was that pupils were often drawn to connect specific problems with math's fundamental regularities.

The American teachers' questions usually asked their pupils to think about the result of a computation ("What answer did you get?"). Their focus on calculation accuracy rarely stepped all the way toward making connections with underlying mathematical rules and regularities.

Here's an interesting finding from eighth-grade classrooms. One study looked at the topics of talk by students and teachers in the math classrooms of four East Asian cities and two Western cities (San Diego, CA, and Melbourne, Australia). The researchers discovered that discussions about *any topic whatsoever* occurred more frequently in the two Western cities. But when they counted *only* the occurrence of key mathematical terms—such as equation, co-planar, and hypotenuse—the East Asian classrooms, and especially those in Shanghai, were ahead of those in the West. Commenting on these findings, they wrote:

> Students in Shanghai had the opportunity to articulate their understanding of key mathematical terms through a structured process of teacher invitation and prompt that built upon the contributions of a sequence of students. Classrooms in Japan provided many instances where a student made the first announcement of a term without specific teacher prompting.[16]

VISITING SIMILAR LESSONS IN JAPAN AND THE UNITED STATES

Before we consider the specific strategies of math teachers in East Asia, let's pause to look in on third-grade math lessons in the United States and Japan.

An American Lesson Introducing Fractions[17]

The teacher announced that today's lesson concerned "fractions." She defined a fraction and wrote a few on the board, in each case pointing out the "numerator" and "denominator." A "quick and snappy" review followed: "What do we call this?" she asked. "And this?" She assured herself that the children understood the meaning of these key terms.

The rest of the lesson was devoted to the teacher's instructing the pupils in applying the rules for forming fractions and in having them work individually at their desks, practicing representative problems.

A Japanese Lesson Introducing Fractions[18]

The lesson wasn't formally introduced. Instead, the teacher held up a large beaker containing colored water. "How many liters of juice do you think are in here?" he asked. The pupils offered various guesses. The teacher suggested that they pour the juice into some one-liter beakers.

Each receiving beaker was divided into thirds by horizontal lines. The juice filled one beaker all the way, plus part of a second beaker. The teacher pointed out that, in the second receiving beaker, the juice came up to the low-est line; only one of its three parts was full.

The teacher revealed a second large beaker with colored water, plus two one-liter beakers with lines dividing each into halves. He repeated the pour-ing procedure, noting that in the second receiving beaker the juice came up to the midline; only one of its two parts was full.

The teacher noted that in the first large beaker, there had been one liter plus one-out-of-three parts of a liter of juice. In the second large beaker, there had been one liter plus one-out-of-two parts of a liter of juice. He wrote 1⅓ and 1½ on the board. Then he asked the pupils to figure out how to represent in writing two parts out of three, two parts out of five, and so forth.

Near the end of the period, the teacher spoke the word "fraction" for the first time. He also introduced the terms "numerator" and "denominator."

This classroom sequence (except for the second juice pouring) can be seen in "The Polished Stones" video beginning at sixteen minutes, twenty seconds.

SPECIFIC STRATEGIES OF MATH
TEACHERS IN EAST ASIA

Among the specific strategies of the teachers are these:

- Beginning with the problem of the day
- Emphasizing abstract/symbolic reasoning
- Insuring coherence; making connections
- Using formal proofs and deductive reasoning.

Beginning with the Problem of the Day

A common feature of mathematics classes in East Asia, including at the sec-ondary level, is that the class begins with the problem of the day.

The problem of the day is not a quiz, drill, review, or homework check. Instead, it's a never-previously-encountered type of problem. It draws on some of what the pupils already know, but it also deliberately exceeds their knowledge, if only slightly.

In Japan,[19] pupils are given up to fifteen minutes to tackle the problem indi-vidually and/or in spontaneously convened groups. The teacher circulates, answering questions in ways that do not obviate the pupils' need to rack their brains to figure out what to do. Teachers believe that

> students learn best by first struggling to solve mathematics problems. Frustra-tion and confusion are taken to be a natural part of the learning process, because each person must struggle with a situation or problem first in order to make sense of the information he or she hears later.[20]

In China,[21] the teacher often begins as well by presenting a challenging problem but without necessarily allowing so much time for the pupils to find ways to solve it. The crucial similarity between Japan and China is that in both cases, the challenge introduced by the initial problem often becomes the main focus of the *entire* lesson.

The videotaped sequence of the problem of the day introduced by the geometry teacher in Taiwan is a fine example of this strategy. A variation on this strategy is seen in the Japanese teacher's beakers with colored water.

Emphasizing Abstract/Symbolic Reasoning

Abstract/symbolic means that, instead of dealing with each new math problem as a unique experience ("concrete"), you begin by trying to recognize the problem as a certain type, that is, as being similar to a type of problem with which you have experience and know how to solve. To do that, you need to have learned to recognize the *essential features* of math problems, which requires abstract thinking. And you need to see that some details of a new problem can be represented by symbols, which will make its solution far more efficient.

The abilities to abstractly perceive the essential features of a never-before-seen problem, to symbolically represent some of its features, and to select from among several alternatives an appropriate method to solve it, are *high-level thinking skills*. "These aims cannot be achieved by rote-drill," observed one research team.[22]

Students in East Asia consistently demonstrate that they have these high-level skills. This can result from only one cause: Teachers prioritize their students' learning to think abstractly and symbolically. The teachers accomplish this through the application of either a conceptual variation or a procedural variation strategy, or both.[23]

Conceptual variation: Mathematical concepts are inherently abstract, but they usually can be introduced in ways that make use of physical objects and visual experiences. The objective is to enable the pupils to mentally connect the abstraction with its real-world embodiments.

Here are two examples: (1) A geometrical concept is "non-coplanar lines," which describes two or more lines that are not on the same plane. The pupils' own desks as well as the classroom's walls and ceiling readily supply examples of contrasting planes and lines. (2) A mathematical concept is "equation," an expression that almost always comprises one or more unknowns and an equal sign. Sometimes teachers introduce several equations (such as $2x = 1$; $4x - 3 = 5$; $x^2 + y^2 = 1$) and encourage pupils to collaborate on finding the common features among them all.

In these and other ways, pupils are helped to recognize the essential features of each concept. They gain the ability, when encountering an unfamiliar problem, to categorize it as being of a certain type, and therefore, to be solvable using procedures that they've previously learned.

Procedural variation: We've already seen that, in East Asia, math teachers often begin classes with a challenging problem, and then expect class members to come up with a variety of ways of finding the answer. In addition, they sometimes lead a class through a step-by-step process for solving a problem, then through different steps for solving the same problem. They introduce more challenging problems of the same type, focusing on the essential feature that calls for a just-learned procedure. They might even lead their pupils through an erroneous process for handling a problem, asking them to figure out at what point the process breaks down, and why.

Insuring Coherence; Making Connections

At the beginning of chapter 5, we noted the astonishing level of effort that teachers in East Asia lavish on their special "Lesson Study" process. Actually, great effort and care go into their planning of *every* lesson, which accounts for their lesson plans being much longer and far more detailed than those of American teachers. Outcomes include that (a) their teaching of math (and other subjects) gains the quality of coherence within each lesson and (b) their pupils learn to perceive the connections among mathematical ideas, facts, and procedures.[24]

Coherence: Coherence within a lesson is attained when the pupils readily perceive that its activities are all related to each other. That's more likely when only one or two main topics are dealt with. One study compared the number of topics in fifth-grade math classes in Taiwan and the United States. Each lesson was divided into five-minute segments and the topics discussed within each were counted. In Taiwan, 55 percent of all segments focused on one topic; in the United States, only 17 percent did.[25]

One reason a tight focus is typical is that the problem of the day becomes the centerpiece of the whole lesson. It's approached from several perspectives, leading to (a) awareness of its essential features and (b) recognition that more than one solution procedure often is applicable. One research team remarked that:

> In Japanese classrooms the students work with few problems consisting of many elements, while in American classrooms the students work with many problems consisting of few elements.[26]

Connections: Some researchers have become convinced that "making connections" is a critical factor in explaining any individual's math superiority.[27]

This means that the person, when encountering a problem, has learned to notice and take into account its conceptual links, that is, its connections among mathematical ideas, facts, procedures, and fundamental regularities. Coherence in a lesson makes it more likely that pupils will have opportunities to recognize one or more connections. This appears to be a priority of math teachers in East Asia.

For example, a teacher whose priority is that her pupils will master procedures might ask them simply to graph three equations, and then check their work. A teacher whose priority is to help pupils make connections might ask them to "graph these three equations *and* examine the role of the numbers in determining the slope of the three associated lines." After the pupils have time to collaborate, she would lead a whole-class discussion about the connections.[28]

The TIMSS 1999 Video Study assessed the United States plus five other countries whose eighth-graders' math achievement had tested much higher than that of their U.S. peers.[29] The researchers wanted to understand the main purpose of the problems being given to students.

They posited that any problem could be given to students to focus on (a) using procedures, (b) stating concepts, or (c) making connections. When they studied the videotapes to count only the making-connections problems, they were surprised to find that the U.S. teachers were similar to teachers in the other five countries: They gave fewer making-connections problems than some, but more than others.

So the researchers posited that any given problem could then be *discussed in class* in a way that prioritized one of those three purposes, plus a fourth: (d) giving results only. They studied the videotapes again. When they counted only the problems that initially had been given for the purpose of "making connections," the U.S. data were jaw-dropping: 92 percent were discussed in terms of giving results or using procedures; 8 percent were discussed in terms of stating concepts. What was the percentage for making connections? Solve for P: $P = 100\% - (92\% + 8\%)$.[30]

Using Formal Proofs and Deductive Reasoning[31]

Mathematics is a body of knowledge that has evolved over millennia, advancing by means of a language of step-by-step reasoning or logical processing known as "deduction,"[32] leading to formal "proofs." A proof occurs when one states an assumption about a mathematical or geometrical relationship, then uses deductive logic to demonstrate, step by step, that the assumption is correct.

Formal mathematical language is taught and expected to be used in East Asian classrooms,[33] but rarely in U.S. classrooms. One study found that U.S.

teachers wanted pupils to *know about* rules in an informal way. But they didn't expect pupils to view rules as separate entities, nor to formally recite any rule during classroom discussions.

Teachers in East Asia took deductive reasoning, rules, and proofs seriously, holding them up as being foundational to mathematics and insisting that pupils formally recite the applicable rule, fully and accurately, as part of each proof:

> *Teacher:* Good. What's your rationale for that conclusion?
> *Pupil 1:* It's based on the rationale of consistent quotient.
> *Teacher:* Can you say that in detail?
> *Pupil 1:* The quotient will stay consistent if two numbers are multiplied or divided by the same number.
> *Teacher:* Sit down, please. Anything else? You, please.
> *Pupil 2:* The quotient will stay consistent if two numbers are multiplied or divided by the same number *at the same time.*
> *Teacher:* Okay, anything else? You, please.
> *Pupil 3:* Except zero.
> *Teacher:* Good. This is a very important condition. We must pay attention to it.[34]

A Malaysian professor who had the opportunity to pay extended visits to Chinese and U.S. primary schools concluded that in the Chinese classrooms, "getting the correct answer wasn't the main goal. It was why, why not, how, what if, and how do you know."[35]

HOW TEACHERS BUILD HIGH-LEVEL THINKING SKILLS

A research team decided to visit first- and fifth-grade classrooms in East Asia and the United States to have a look at how teachers were trying to develop high-level mathematical thinking skills.

The team selected a wide range of primary schools in China, Taiwan, Japan, and the United States, and in each school they selected two first-grade and two fifth-grade classrooms for painstaking observation.[36]

The team reasoned that, for pupils to be "actively" learning, they had to be actively engaged. So they counted the number of lessons during which one or more *pupils*, not the teacher,[37]

(a) *explained* a mathematical concept or procedure;
(b) *evaluated* the relevance or correctness of another pupil's answer.

The researchers' findings are summarized in Table 7.2.

Table 7.2

(a) Percentage of Classes in which Pupils Explained Mathematics							
First Grade				Fifth Grade			
China	Taiwan	Japan	U.S.	China	Taiwan	Japan	U.S.
98.7%	89.6%	89.6%	69.7%	100.0%	93.7%	98.7%	80.4%

(b) Percentage of Classes in which Pupils Evaluated Answers							
First Grade				Fifth Grade			
China	Taiwan	Japan	U.S.	China	Taiwan	Japan	U.S.
61.3%	69.6%	70.4%	31.4%	63.2%	65.0%	62.5%	52.7%

Source: Shin-ying Lee (1998). Mathematics learning and teaching in the school context: Reflections from cross-cultural comparisons. *Global Prospects for Education: Development, Culture, and Schooling*. Based on table 1, p. 55.

The team noticed that American teachers usually called on pupils who volunteered. Teachers in East Asia called on pupils whether or not they volunteered. "Not knowing who the teacher will call on next, all students must be actively engaged in the thinking process," they wrote.[38]

In addition, the team wanted to understand how teachers stimulate pupils to understand concepts and build relationships and connections. So they counted the number of lessons during which the teacher[39]

(c) *used a variety of examples*—word problems, computations, diagrams, and/or tangible manipulatives—to illustrate a single new concept;

(d) *extended pupils' answers* by adding new comments or questions, such as by asking for additional ways of solving the same problem;

(e) *related a solution procedure to abstract concepts* that underlie that procedure and can be generalized to solve similar problems;

(f) *elicited sophisticated answers from pupils*, for example, answers involving concepts, equations, deductions, or explanations that addressed "how" and "why."

The researchers' findings are summarized in Table 7.3.

Also reported within these fifth-grade data for eliciting sophisticated answers was a comparison that revealed a yawning East-West gap: the frequency with which teachers asked pupils to respond by providing a mathematical equation.

In more than 60 percent of the Japanese and Chinese classes, and in more than 40 percent of the Taiwanese classes, students expressed their thinking using a mathematical equation. But this occurred in only 8 percent of the American fifth-grade classes.[40]

Table 7.3

(c) Percentage of Classes in which Teachers Used a Variety of Examples							
First Grade				Fifth Grade			
China	Taiwan	Japan	U.S.	China	Taiwan	Japan	U.S.
76.3%	74.2%	46.3%	28.9%	55.3%	47.1%	47.5%	30.4%

(d) Percentage of Classes in which Teachers Extended Pupils' Answers							
First Grade				Fifth Grade			
China	Taiwan	Japan	U.S.	China	Taiwan	Japan	U.S.
37.5%	41.3%	33.8%	7.9%	71.1%	22.5%	57.5%	22.7%

(e) Percentage of Classes in which Teachers Related Procedures to Concepts							
First Grade				Fifth Grade			
China	Taiwan	Japan	U.S.	China	Taiwan	Japan	U.S.
53.8%	31.3%	49.6%	18.0%	73.7%	37.9%	52.5%	24.6%

(f) Percentage of Classes in which Teachers Elicited Sophisticated Answers							
First Grade				Fifth Grade			
China	Taiwan	Japan	U.S.	China	Taiwan	Japan	U.S.
43.8%	52.9%	26.3%	2.8%	68.4%	20.0%	22.5%	13.3%

Source: Shin-ying Lee (1998). Mathematics learning and teaching in the school context: Reflections from cross-cultural comparisons. *Global Prospects for Education: Development, Culture, and Schooling*. Based on table 2, p. 57.

The comparisons reported above support the oft-repeated contention that American primary school pupils encounter fewer opportunities to gain high-level mathematical thinking skills than their peers in the schools of China, Taiwan, and Japan.

A MIRROR FOR AMERICANS

As we look into the mirror of East Asian schooling, what do we notice about *our* schools and the values *we* apply when thinking about them?

- **How mathematics lessons are delivered:** Four factors account for the success of East Asian mathematics teaching:

1. *The teachers*, who are thoroughly prepared to teach each lesson.
2. *The pupils*, who arrive at school with an inner drive to learn.

3. *The knowledge*, which is revered, as are pupils' dogged efforts to master it.
4. *The values and assumptions* that underlie the public's expectations about how to transfer essential knowledge to pupils.

In East Asia, most people value in children and adults a capacity for persevering effort and a willingness to endure frustrating struggles to attain worthwhile objectives. They assume that children can be intrigued by a math problem with a never-before-seen feature or by a new concept that captures an aspect of the real world. They believe children will be drawn to tackle a challenge if they can initially try to figure out, on their own, ways to overcome it. They expect teachers to directively facilitate children's comprehension of the processes *and* the foundational concepts of mathematics.

And they *do not* think such knowledge must be doled out in tiny, failure-proof steps.

In my view, these factors give students in East Asia a competitive edge and help to account for their superior performances on the international mathematics tests. These factors are about cultural values and assumptions, deeply intertwined features of East Asian societies that are beyond the reach of our individualistic mindset.

But wait. Don't some of those teachers' *specific strategies* warrant our attention?

FURTHER READING

If you'd like more detail about the researchers' findings, or simply wish to know what inspired the contents of chapter 7, read these entries in the annotated bibliography at www.amirrorforamericans.info.

- Becker, Jerry P., Toshio Sawada, & Yoshinori Shimizu (1999), Some findings of the U.S.-Japan cross-cultural research on students' problem-solving behaviors.
- Cai, Jinfa, & Victor Cifarelli (2004), Thinking mathematically by Chinese learners: A cross-national comparative perspective.
- Cai, Jinfa (2005), U.S. and Chinese teachers' constructing, knowing, and evaluating representations to teach mathematics.
- Clark, David, & Li Hua Xu (2008), Distinguishing between mathematics classrooms in Australia, China, Japan, Korea, and the United States.
- Gu, Lingyuan, Rongjin Huang, & Ference Marton (2004), Teaching with variation: A Chinese way of promoting effective mathematics learning.

- Hess, Robert D., & Hiroshi Azuma (1991), Cultural support for schooling: Contrasts between Japan and the United States.
- Hiebert, James, et al. (2005), Mathematics teaching in the United States today (and tomorrow): Results from the TIMSS 1999 Video Study.
- Kawanaka, Takako, James W. Stigler, & James Hiebert (1999), Studying mathematics classrooms in Germany, Japan, and the United States.
- Lee, Shin-ying (1998), Mathematics learning and teaching in the school context: Reflections from cross-cultural comparisons.
- Lim, Chap Sam (2007), Characteristics of mathematics teaching in Shanghai, China: Through the lens of a Malaysian.
- Linn, Marcia C., et al. (2000), Beyond fourth-grade science: Why do U.S. and Japanese students diverge?
- Mok, Ida, & Paul Morris (2001), The metamorphosis of the "virtuoso": Pedagogic patterns in Hong Kong primary mathematics classrooms.
- Mok, Ida Ah Chee(2006), Shedding light on the East Asian learner paradox: Reconstructing student-centeredness in a Shanghai classroom.
- Perry, Michelle (2000), Explanation of mathematical concepts in Japanese, Chinese, and U.S. first- and fifth-grade classrooms.
- Schleppenbach, Meg, et al. (2007), The answer is only the beginning: Extended discourse in Chinese and U.S. mathematics classrooms.
- Sekiguchi, Yasuhiro, & Mikio Miyazaki (2000), Argumentation and mathematical proof in Japan.
- Shimizu, Yoshinori (1999), Aspects of mathematics teacher education in Japan: Focusing on teachers' roles.
- Stevenson, Harold W., & James W. Stigler (1992), *The Learning Gap*.
- Stigler, James W., & Harold W. Stevenson (1991), How Asian teachers polish each lesson to perfection.
- Stigler, James W., Clea Fernandez, & Makoto Yoshida (1998), Cultures of mathematics instruction in Japanese and American classrooms.
- Stigler, James W., & James Hiebert (1999), *The Teaching Gap*.
- Stigler, James W., & James Hiebert (2004), Improving mathematics teaching.
- Usui, Hiroshi (1996), Differences in teacher classroom behaviors in the United States and Japan: A field note.
- Wang, Tao, & John Murphy (2004), An examination of coherence in a Chinese mathematics classroom.
- Zhang, Dianzhou, Shiqi Li, & Ruifen Tang (2004), The "Two Basics": Mathematics teaching and learning in mainland China.

Chapter 8

East Asian Primary Schools, Part III
Other Performance-Related Topics

> Whereas I, too, entered Japan completely against "drill and kill" methods of instruction, I left appreciating the value of such repetition for mastering the basic skills as part of one's body, freeing the mind to achieve greater levels of creativity and accomplishment.
>
> American researcher Nancy E. Sato[1]

If you've read this book all the way to here, you've gained a better grasp of the constellation of elements in East Asian classrooms that contribute to the consistently high academic performance of young people there.

A key element in East Asian primary school classrooms is the pupils themselves. They are the subject of *The Drive to Learn*, which discusses how their parents raise them, infusing them with a passionate drive to learn—including to learn academic subjects in classrooms. There's reason to believe that the academic superiority of pupils across East Asia is explained at least as much by their upbringing at home as it is by the education they receive in schools.

The subject of *this* book is the education those pupils receive in schools. Clearly, it is another major contributor to their high levels of academic achievement. We've covered a great deal in the previous seven chapters. But a few topics remain that were either mentioned only briefly or that didn't fit into the previous chapters. We need to address these remaining topics to complete the portrait of how Chinese and Japanese pupils are taught and why they learn so well. We'll do so under these headings:

MORE ABOUT THE KNOWLEDGE
- Textbooks: Appearance and Use
- The Importance of the Basics

MORE ABOUT CLASSROOM PROCESS
 * The Sequence of Learning Activities
 * Asking Questions
 * Patterns of Feedback and Discussion

CONSTRUCTIVISM EAST AND WEST
 * Constructivism versus Instructivism
 * Social Constructivism and Scaffolding
 * Constructivism in the United States and East Asia

MORE ABOUT THE KNOWLEDGE

Textbooks: Appearance and Use

If you held an East Asian textbook in your hands and flipped through it for a
minute, you might not be certain what you were looking at.

Our textbooks are large, thick, and heavy; theirs are small, slim, and light.
Ours are hardcover; theirs are paperback. Ours are loaded with full-color
illustrations, design flourishes, and special features; theirs have some black-
and-white illustrations and, well, that's about it.

A one-minute video nicely illustrates this difference. On YouTube, search
for "Useless Textbooks in Canada and Japan" (duration 1:04).

Here's the thing: Both China and Japan have a national curriculum, which
sounds forbiddingly massive, but which dictates only learning goals—*not*
methods, *not* lessons—for each subject area and grade. For a textbook to be
approved by the ministry, it must cover all content mandated in its subject/
grade section of the national curriculum. Each subject/grade section is narrowly focused, which is reflected in the textbooks; for example, in Japan, the
textbook for eighth-grade science covers eight topics, compared with sixty-
five for a typical American eighth-grade science text![2]

In chapter 6 it was noted that teachers in East Asia are thoroughly familiar
with their pupils' textbooks. Here's why: they efficiently cover *every* goal—
no more, no less—required by the national curriculum and include explanations and examples. They're useful!

Several studies have compared East Asian and American texts.[3] In most
cases, the findings are tedious to read. But one study overviews the main contrasts. Compared were eighth-grade math textbooks from East Asia (including Korea) with those from both the United States and England.

In East Asian texts, each chapter is titled according to a mathematical strand
such as "Equations," "Functions," and "Probability," and each is composed of
homogeneous content within that strand. One strand is covered in one chapter

only. Western texts have modules with themes such as "Making Choices," "Sea Life," and "Search and Rescue." Each module has sections in which heterogeneous concepts are introduced (e.g., algebra, functions, and statistics all within a module). One strand is usually repeated over several modules.

East Asian texts have a limited number of features, concentrating on explanations, examples, and exercises. Western texts have a variety of features—projects, application exercises, technology, self-assessments, and career connections—that are rarely found in East Asian texts.

In East Asian texts, concepts are introduced before examples are given. Great weight is given to the mathematical content itself, which demands effort on the part of the students. Western texts first present various introductory activities and explorations that are supposed to set the content in a realistic context; these serve as "scaffolding" that allows students to familiarize themselves with new concepts step by step.

But the context is not always effectively related to the concepts. In the "Search and Rescue" module, the story is told of a boy in a small plane when the pilot has a heart attack and the plane crashes. This introduces the concept of angle—vertex, ray, acute angle, etc.—which is only vaguely, even confusingly, related to the context (the story).

East Asian texts force students to learn the noble logical system of mathematics by presenting a combination of concepts, symbols, and algorithms in a decontextualized way. Western texts see math as a human endeavor that needs to be learned "in context," its abstract concepts "dressed up" in realistic situations. However, when the scaffolding process is only vaguely related to the content of mathematics, sooner or later students will have to face the hard math that's concealed under the comfortable fancy outlook.[4]

The Importance of The Basics[5]

In chapter 3 we encountered "kata," which was discussed in terms of the correct *process* of learning something. Individual learners "enter through form," which is supplied to the learner by someone who's already mastered the skill, art form, or knowledge domain in question.

To people in East Asia, learning isn't only about a superior learning process; it's also about valuable content. And regardless of the content you're learning, what you master *first* is its foundational knowledge—a.k.a. The Basics.

The belief is that foundational knowledge is exactly what that term implies: a firm *foundation* for the more practical and imaginative topics that potentially will follow. Securely laying that foundation is of the utmost importance for all the learning that follows.

Recall the story of Howard Gardner's small son, Benjamin, who was flailing away at trying to deposit a pendant-attached key into the slot while his trial-and-error-tolerant parents looked on. Typically, a Chinese person nearby would come over, grasp Benjamin's hand in her own, then gently but firmly guide it to the slot, orient the pendant just so, and deposit the key. It's an eye-arm-hand coordination skill, The Basic skill for the complex movement skills yet to be learned.

Within each domain of knowledge, learning The Basics is not an end goal, but rather the first way station. It is the indispensable *first step* of a far longer process of mastering any body of knowledge worth learning. On the steady foundation of The Basics, then, the learner can begin constructing the edifice—at least the learner who intends to move beyond being a novice or dilettante.

Given that The Basics lay the foundation for all that follows, it's best to learn them efficiently and effectively: efficiently so that one can move beyond this initial stage without undue delay; effectively so that one can *rely on them for support* as he or she moves on to more interesting, applicable, complicated and, yes, creative learning and performing.

To the East Asian mind, an efficient *and* effective learning process calls for a straightforward, no-frills process of imitation and repetition to the point of overlearning. Once overlearned, The Basics are always retained, always ready in mental memory (and, often, muscle memory) to be quickly brought into service as the heights of learning are scaled.

No doubt the phrase "imitation and repetition" has a few readers blanching. Yes, that means drills. They are efficient. They are effective. Americans calmly accept—no, they insist on—endless physical drills for youth who intend to be highfliers in sports. Why not also mental drills for those whose aim is to become highfliers in one of the STEM[6] subjects?

MORE ABOUT CLASSROOM PROCESS

The Sequence of Learning Activities[7]

Related to the importance of The Basics are East Asian beliefs about the appropriate sequencing of classroom learning activities, which contrast with the beliefs of many American educators.

In the United States, pupils are expected to become actively involved with new content quickly, often as soon as it's introduced. Known by rubrics such as "learning by doing" and "discovery learning," pupils are given time to figure out unfamiliar material for themselves, or are asked for their ideas or opinions about it, or even are asked to put the material to immediate use. The belief is that it's better for children to learn new skills and knowledge experientially instead of having new things authoritatively presented. Among Americans, the process of active exploration, discovery, and creation is highly admired, more so than the drudgery of painstakingly acquiring knowledge or a skill under an acknowledged expert's guidance (unless, of course, it's sports related).

In other words, the learning step of "application" or "demonstration" occurs *before* the learning step of "skill acquisition." Most people in East Asia believe that's the wrong way 'round, for it puts learners in the uncomfortable position of having to publicly reveal their lack of capability before they've had an extended opportunity to study, understand, practice, and develop competence in the new material.

This difference in sequencing is most clearly observed when Western ESL or EFL[8] teachers show up in East Asia to help the locals learn to speak English via the method called Communicative Language Teaching or CLT. The idea behind CLT is that learners will acquire English *by using it* beginning on Day One: Jump right in; talk out loud; don't worry about errors. For most people in East Asia, this is an abhorrent strategy! They expect a teacher to model correct English, to use drills and choral responses for practicing words and phrases, to allow time away from class (evenings, weekends) for practice—*and only then* to ask students to individually speak aloud in public the material they've been trying to master in private. And when students do so, they confidently expect their teacher to correct their errors openly, immediately, and authoritatively.[9]

People in East Asia consider trial-and-error learning *during a classroom lesson* to be a serious waste of precious time with the teacher, their bearer of authoritative knowledge. (Trial-and-error during private study is another matter.) It's much more satisfying and efficient to begin with expert guidance and modeling, to strive in private for understanding and competence, and *only then* to demonstrate one's newly acquired skill in public.

Asking Questions

When question-asking during East Asian lessons was previously discussed, the focus was mainly on the characteristics of teacher-posed questions. You'll recall that they usually ask open-ended questions, the type that call for a long, thoughtful response, which can lead to "sticky probing." Math teachers, for instance, tend to ask open-ended "how?" and "why?" questions, plus questions that call for displaying one's command of underlying mathematical rules.

A good example of an open-ended question is the "problem of the day" posed at the start of a lesson, which is intended to raise pupils' active curiosity about a topic. "Active" because they're given up to fifteen minutes to discuss possible answers. It's also an example of a "naïve question," so-called because the teacher pretends to not know the answer. A science teacher might begin with, "Isn't it strange that iodine on all potatoes grown in three different conditions changed color? That means . . . ,"[10] at which point she asks the pupils to discuss among themselves the possible reasons for this curious phenomenon.

Pupil-posed questions came up in chapter 6 in connection with the religious service analogy: The pupils' role is to never interrupt, never jump in with a question about something they didn't "get." But this analogy falls short because it allows people to imagine that primary school teachers in East Asia "lecture" to pupils who are "passive" listeners, which is false.

That analogy helped to portray "whole-class interactive learning," which acquired its name because it involves a great deal of interactivity under the teacher's carefully prepared direction. During vigorous whole-class discussions, pupils do ask questions. But in general, teachers are expected to anticipate lesson elements that pupils will find difficult and to present those in a way that will make questions unnecessary.

In chapter 1, Americans' stereotypical belief about East Asian classrooms was mentioned. Part of it is that "students never ask questions." This stereotype likely arose from accounts circulated by Western observers and faculty members in East Asian high school and university classrooms. From *that* perspective, it's accurate: *during class*, students at those academic levels rarely ask questions.

Table 8.1 compares expectations about student question-asking at the high school and university levels in the United States and East Asia.

Table 8.1 Expectations about Question-Asking by Older Students

In the United States	In East Asia
An individual student	An individual student or a study group[11]
asks a question as soon as it occurs to him or her (or very soon after), that is,	asks a question after trying to find an answer via reflection or between-classes research, that is,
while the teacher is busy teaching or otherwise involved with the class.	when the teacher is *not* involved with the class; therefore, very rarely while class is in session.
The question is spoken aloud so that the student's classmates hear it, and	The question often is posed at a time and place that's out of earshot of classmates, and
is addressed directly to the teacher	is usually addressed directly to the teacher[12]
to inquire about something just said that the student didn't understand, or	to inquire about something said during a previous class that wasn't understood, *but*
to dispute one of the teacher's statements (or a statement made by a classmate).	*never* to dispute one of the teacher's statements. (Classmates' statements may be debated.)

Table by Cornelius N. Grove.

In East Asia, question-asking by older students often begins in the corridor after the class session ends; teachers know that they need to delay their departure from the area. Sometimes, a student or a study group will arrange to meet the teacher at another time and place[13], at which time thoughtful extended discussions are likely to occur because the student or the study group has already devoted effort trying to find the answer and has become relatively knowledgeable about the topic.

Patterns of Feedback and Discussion

To sharpen the portrayal of whole-class interactive learning, it's important to explore more deeply into feedback and discussion patterns during East Asian lessons.

Noticeably in scarce supply is praise.[14] Children are rarely praised in private or public—including by their parents—but they are frequent recipients of directive guidance, criticism, negative feedback, and punishments. Neither good academic performance nor good behavior is deemed routinely praiseworthy. It's expected. When it occurs, life is proceeding normally. So what's to discuss?

One veteran classroom researcher commented that

Praise serves to cut off discussion and highlight the teacher's role as the authority regarding what's correct and incorrect. It encourages children to be satisfied with their performance rather than informing them about where they need improvement.[15]

A Japanese elementary school teacher put the matter succinctly: "Praise children for good behavior? I think it's demeaning."[16]

Students who behave badly—yes, there are some—are referred to the discipline teacher, which may result in demerits, extra assignments, standing in class, or writing improving statements repeatedly on the board. Poor academic performance is likely to result in negative feedback from the teacher. "If followed by appropriate explanations and guidance, this may have a positive effect of motivating students to work harder," concluded one researcher.[17]

What about the pupils' self-esteem? Concern about self-esteem is an American preoccupation; it's barely on the radar screens of East Asians. Researchers studying mothers in the United States and Taiwan found that there was no word in either Chinese or Taiwanese[18] that meant "self-esteem"; they settled for "self-confidence-heart/mind." Mothers in the United States "could not talk about childrearing without talking about self-esteem." Only a few of the mothers in Taiwan even mentioned self-confidence-heart/

mind—and when they did, they were wary! They did *not* want their child to have much of it. Their belief was that it leads to "frustration in the face of failure, stubbornness, and unwillingness to listen and be corrected."[19]

Finally, let's revisit teacher-led discussions. As noted in chapter 6, a typical pattern in the United States is for the teacher to ask short-answer questions, calling on one or more volunteers. If an answer is correct, the teacher offers praise. If it's incorrect, the teacher either offers praise ("Good try!") or calls on another volunteer. Note that (a) there's *a lot* of praise, (b) answers almost always come from volunteers, and (c) the teacher is the sole decider between right and wrong. One observer said without irony that American teachers reminded him of quiz show hosts.[20]

Most teachers in East Asia offer praise *only* when a pupil's response is exceptionally good; otherwise, the teacher moves on. If a response is wrong, here's where it gets interesting. The teacher occasionally says, "No, that's wrong." More likely is that she will call on a sequence of pupils—*rarely* volunteers—to decide whether it's wrong, to analyze why it's wrong, and to state the implications of its being wrong. So after the initial question-and-answer exchange, subsequent exchanges often find the teacher asking things like, "Is his answer correct?" "Where's the mistake?" "Can you expand on what she said?"

> This means that the pupils involved in the second exchange must have listened to the first, and the first pupil must listen to the second, since they are likely to be asked to repeat or comment on the second exchange in a third one. Any pupil can be called on for the second exchange, or sometimes a third, fourth, or fifth exchange, each expanding on, repeating, or evaluating the preceding ones. Since pupils stand to speak and such cycles are high paced, pupils are physically and verbally involved.[21]

CONSTRUCTIVISM EAST AND WEST[22]

Constructivism versus Instructivism

Here's how our own American authority on schooling, Dr. Diane Ravitch, explains constructivism in her glossary of educational terms:

> Constructivism is based on the belief that students learn by constructing their own knowledge. Its methods center on exploration, hands-on experience, inquiry, self-paced learning, peer teaching, and discussion. Constructivists suggest that only knowledge that one works through oneself is truly integrated and understood. Constructivism is identified with inquiry learning, discovery

learning, student-centered instruction, and other forms in which the teacher minimizes Direct Instruction.[23]

That's constructivism as it's conceived of here in the United States. As would be expected in any highly individualistic culture, there's heavy reliance on the student as a veritable Lone Ranger who gets learning done pretty much all by himself, with little direct instruction.

"Direct instruction" is a method in which the teacher explains the purpose of what will be taught and presents the content in an orderly way, with students contributing verbally largely by responding to the teacher's questions.[24] Teachers' questions often are the kind that enables them to determine if the students understood the new content. This approach is also known as "instructivism."

Clearly, constructivism and instructivism are grounded in two sharply contrasting understandings of how children learn best. Proponents of each tend to be dismissive of those of the opposite persuasion. Currently here in the United States, the constructivist view enjoys many admirers, being closely associated with progressive education.[25]

When progressives want to be dismissive of East Asian education, they claim that it's instructivist (although they rarely use that term, which never gained wide use) or traditional. But as shown herein, hundreds of research studies have shown that East Asian primary school classrooms are *not* instructivist.

Social Constructivism and Scaffolding[26]

We need also to take note of "social constructivism," a view of how children learn based on the work of Russian psychologist Lev Vygotsky (1896–1934). Vygotsky had dozens of insightful ideas about learning, communication, and children's development. Here's an overview of one slice of this seminal thinker's wide range of ideas.

Each newborn, observed Vygotsky, arrives into the company of parents and others who are participating in the social and cultural milieu of their time and place. From them the infant gains familiarity with relationships and objects, knowledge and myths, processes and norms, all handed down from earlier generations.

A young child's mental and social capacities don't develop in isolation. They develop while immersed in meanings and practices *that enter the child's mind via social interactions with others*. As these ideas gradually become internalized and familiar, they take root in the child's own mind, expanding, shaping, and fine-tuning his inborn cognitive capacities.

Vygotsky noted that there's a huge range of activities and tasks that children must learn how to perform: how to use utensils, greet honored guests, pronounce difficult words, herd sheep or use a smartphone (or both!), count and add. At first, each is utterly unfamiliar. Gradually, children recognize that there are patterns and purposes in what others nearby are doing. They begin making halting attempts to do likewise.

At any point in time, there are tasks that are too challenging to be mastered alone, but that *can* be acquired with the guidance of adults or more-skilled children. Vygotsky gave a name to those tasks that the child can't yet learn on his own *but can learn with expert help*: the "zone of proximal development." Here's Vygotsky's own explanation:

> The zone of proximal development defines those functions that have not yet matured but are in the process of maturation, functions that will mature soon but are currently in an embryonic state. These functions could be termed the "buds" or "flowers" of development rather than the "fruits" of development. A child's actual developmental level characterizes mental development retrospectively, while the zone of proximal development characterizes mental development prospectively.[27]

Vygotsky referenced the work of an American researcher who showed that among children aged three to five there were two levels of ability: tasks they can perform on their own and tasks they can learn to perform in collaboration with one another or under adult guidance.[28] That second group of tasks is the children's zone of proximal development.

After Vygotsky drew attention to the guidance that more-skilled others provide, directive and supportive assistance of this type became known as "scaffolding." Scaffolding is much discussed among educators here and abroad, including progressives. Here's part of Ravitch's definition:

> Coaching or modeling provided by a teacher to increase students' likelihood of success as they develop new skills or learn new concepts. Effective scaffolding occurs when the teacher explains an assignment, brings the task to an appropriate level of difficulty, breaks the task into a doable sequence of operations, provides feedback, and helps students gain mastery of new knowledge.[29]

Note that this definition emphasizes a teacher's directly assisting the children in grasping the "how" of the task by (a) preparing her presentation of the task in readily understood ways and (b) modeling, coaching, and explaining the steps involved (which might involve recalling skills previously learned). A warm, caring, and patient manner is called for, of course, but in no way is scaffolding solely about motivating and encouraging.

Now *that* sounds like good teaching! But hold on. Where's that student Lone Ranger who gets learning done pretty much all by herself?

Constructivism in the United States and East Asia

Having read and pondered hundreds of research reports on East Asian classroom learning, I can say with confidence that "constructivism" *as defined by Diane Ravitch* is not what's occurring in primary schools there.

It's equally clear that "instructivism" is not what's occurring there, either. (But as young people in East Asia advance toward the high school level, instructivism increasingly becomes apt, especially for the more academically inclined students who will face grueling exams.)

The most appropriate generalization about East Asian primary school learning is "social constructivism." Ravitch doesn't define this term, but her definition of scaffolding works quite nicely for social constructivism. Or, we could consider a shorter definition, such as

Social constructivism is about the learning made possible for an individual through his or her interactions with other individuals and groups.[30]

American educational researchers have been interested in social constructivism for some time.[31] They've concluded that a child's learning isn't fostered *only* during early life through interactions with parents and other caretakers, but also during the school years by in-class discussions. Teacher-guided classroom debates and discussions benefit children not only in terms of comprehending the material more fully but also of developing their social skills.

In the foregoing chapters, we've seen that East Asian lessons feature a great deal of on-topic verbal interaction, more than is characteristic of American classrooms. One major research effort (not involving East-West comparisons) found that the typical American teacher spends *less than three minutes per hour* allowing students to talk about ideas with one another and the teacher![32]

Recall little Benjamin's eagerness to put the key through the slot. His level of development didn't enable him to do that. But with help from hotel staff who took his hand in theirs, he could begin mastering that movement earlier than if he'd been left to figure it out himself. Simple eye-arm-hand coordination was within his zone of proximal development; scaffolding was enabling him to move successfully into that zone. That's a simple example of social constructivism in action.

Had the hotel staff not scaffolded Benjamin's efforts, he would have continued to flail away, trial-and-error, for additional days or weeks. His

American parents didn't want to guide his hand; their idea of good learning was aligned with the Lone Ranger, do-it-yourself view of constructivism, as defined by Ravitch at the beginning of this section.

A MIRROR FOR AMERICANS

As we look into the mirror of East Asian schooling, what do we notice about *our* schools and the values *we* apply when thinking about them?

- **The knowledge:** The ways in which people in East Asia respond to knowledge is similar to American ways in some respects, but different in many others. Most people in East Asia hold knowledge—especially the kind passed down by wise forebears and now found in books—in far higher esteem than we do.[33] It's said that in China of old, when someone found a scrap of paper with writing on it, they'd pick it up and preserve it. It's unlikely that occurs nowadays, but the awe with which academic knowledge is regarded remains.

  One contemporary outcome is that East Asian textbooks directly focus on the knowledge to be learned—straight up, no frills. It need not be cloaked in features that make it attractive and engaging to young people. Americans seem to assume that knowledge is like foul-tasting medicine; we'd better conceal it inside something tasty.

  Another outcome is that people in East Asia expect that the first step in learning any skill, art form, or knowledge domain is mastery of its foundational elements. Our disinclination to do likewise is almost certainly due to our belief that mastering The Basics involves drudge-work—you know, "drill and kill"—a foul-tasting medicine if ever there was one! In this case, though, it's impossible to conceal with sweet stuff the drudgery that insures mastery. So we leave The Basics poorly learned and move on, reassuring ourselves that "they can always look it up on their smartphones."

- **Classroom processes:** Repeatedly in this book, we have seen that researchers have found that knowledge-centered discussions among teachers and pupils constantly occur during East Asian lessons. I said "*knowledge-centered* discussions" because some comparative studies have found that there's *more talk* during U.S. lessons—about all sorts of things, often including the knowledge. The evidence is abundant that American pupils, compared with their East Asian peers, are *less likely* to be asked to (a) respond to "how" and "why" questions, (b) explain concepts and procedures to their classmates, or (c) identify errors and diagnose faulty reasoning; as well as being less likely to (d) engage in lengthy discussions about new topics among themselves (not just two-way with the teacher).

Let's face it: The processes of classroom lessons here in the United States simply *do not immerse pupils in the knowledge to be learned* to the same extent as do classroom lessons in East Asia.

- **Constructivism:** Ravitch's Lone Ranger definition of constructivism does not describe what's going on in East Asian primary schools. But Vygotsky-inspired *social constructivism* (learning via one's interactions with others) does provide a good characterization of East Asian primary school lesson processes. It works well in East Asia because of the two factors reviewed in the previous two bullet points, both of which refer to the central role of the knowledge to be learned. A third factor is that (as discussed in *The Drive to Learn*) children in East Asia arrive at the schoolhouse door with more receptivity to classroom learning than American children.

Americans' relatively indifferent attitude toward academic knowledge isn't going to change. Therefore, neither will our children's comparatively lukewarm receptivity toward book-learning in classrooms. It's all just too ingrained in our cultural DNA.

Surely, though, it's possible to make changes as to the central factor in American primary school lessons. Surely we can leverage our new awareness of the centrality of knowledge in East Asian lessons to inspire fresh thinking about how *the knowledge to be learned*, rather than anything about individual pupils, could become the central factor here in the United States, too.

FURTHER READING

If you'd like more detail about the researchers' findings, or simply wish to know what inspired the contents of chapter 8, read these entries in the annotated bibliography at www.amirrorforamericans.info.

- Biggs, John B. (2001), Teaching across cultures.
- Cortazzi, Martin (1998), Learning from Asian lessons: Cultural expectations and classroom talk.
- Cortazzi, Martin, & Lixian Jin (1996), Cultures of learning: Language classrooms in China.
- Frkovich, Ann (2015), Taking it with you: Teacher education and the baggage of cultural dialogue.
- Hu, Guangwei (2002), Potential cultural resistance to pedagogical imports.

- Jin, Lixian, & Martin Cortazzi (1998), Dimensions of dialogue: Large classes in China.
- Li, Yeping (2007), Curriculum and culture: An exploratory examination of mathematics curriculum materials in their system and cultural contexts.
- Linn, Marcia C., et al. (2000), Beyond fourth-grade science: Why do U.S. and Japanese students diverge?
- Ouyang, Huhua (2003), Resistance to the communicative method of language instruction within a progressive Chinese university.
- Paine, Lynn W. (1990), The teacher as virtuoso: A Chinese model for teaching.
- Park, Kyungmee, & Frederick Koon Shing Leung (2006), A comparative study of the mathematics textbooks of China, England, Japan, Korea, and the United States.
- Pratt, Daniel D., Mavis Kelly, & Winnie Wong (1999), Chinese conceptions of "effective teaching" in Hong Kong.
- Rao, Nirmala, et al. (2009), Preschool pedagogy: A fusion of traditional Chinese beliefs and contemporary notions of appropriate practice.
- Salili, Farideh (2001), Teacher-student interaction: Attributional implications and effectiveness of teachers' evaluative feedback.
- Stevenson, Harold, & Shin-ying Lee (1990), Contexts of achievement: A study of American, Chinese, and Japanese children.
- Stigler, James W., & Harold W. Stevenson (1991), How Asian teachers polish each lesson to perfection.
- Tsuchida, Ineko, & Catherine C. Lewis (1998), Responsibility and learning: Some preliminary hypotheses about Japanese elementary classrooms.
- Usui, Hiroshi (1996), Differences in teacher classroom behaviors in the United States and Japan: A field note.
- Zhu, Yan, & Lianghuo Fan (2006), Focus on the representation of problem types in intended curriculum.

Chapter 9

Knowledge-Centered Lessons

Greater time on task is not the primary basis for the high achievement
of Chinese and Japanese children. Instead, its primary basis is the high
quality of the experiences that fill this time.

Harold W. Stevenson and Shin-ying Lee[1]

During our lifetimes, researchers have observed hundreds of primary school
classrooms in East Asia. Would they agree that they were mostly teacher-
centered? Many would answer that query something like this: "Teacher-
centered? Sort of . . . But not in the way we've been thinking about it . . .
Well, they're not exactly student-centered either."

In this chapter, we'll do some "sticky probing" about the meaning of
teacher-centered and student-centered, especially as those terms apply to lesson delivery. And we'll learn why *knowledge-centered* is the best generalization for describing primary school lessons in East Asia.

LABELING CLASSES STUDENT-
OR TEACHER-CENTERED

What is the meaning of student- or child-centered? Diane Ravitch's *Glossary*
explains those terms this way: Classroom activities are "determined by the
interests, characteristics, and needs of the students,"[2] who are "expected to
choose their own learning goals and activities."[3]

In the United States, only a few private schools seriously attempt this
approach. Nevertheless, many educators and parents sing the praises of child-
centered learning, probably because their sense of its meaning doesn't align
with Ravitch's. Most likely, they have in mind classrooms where teachers do

their best to create a learning environment that resonates with each child's unique characteristics.[4]

What does teacher-centered mean? Ravitch says that it designates "a classroom in which the teacher is in charge and makes all the important decisions; also known as the *teacher-dominated classroom*."[5]

Note that, for Americans, "to dominate" is not an admirable activity.

We've been considering these labels within our familiar American context. Several researchers wondered how East Asian and American classrooms compare in terms of student- and teacher-centeredness. Their findings shocked many. Two studies suggested that American classrooms are *more teacher-centered* than those in Japan; two others proposed that Chinese classrooms are *more student-centered* than those in the United States. Let's have a look.

Are U.S. or Japanese Classrooms More Teacher-Centered?

In the first of these two studies,[6] the author was an American anthropologist doing research in Japan who became impressed with the quality of teacher-student relationships there.

She argued that Americans are mistaken to condemn Japanese classrooms as hostile to individual needs. Relationships there are grounded in *emotional connectedness*. Teachers comprehend "whole" pupils by entering their minds and hearts and developing emotional bonds. Divergent thinking is encouraged as teachers ask their pupils to generate solutions to challenging problems. Teachers' authority is muted; pupils have internalized a standard of behavior based on empathy with their classmates. Teachers sidestep the role of arbiter of right and wrong. And all pupils are treated similarly; in Japanese primary schools, tracking very rarely occurs.[7]

She compared all that with what's going in the United States:

> The American classroom relies heavily on teachers' assessments of individual abilities, developmental readiness, and disciplinary control. Emotional well-being and social skills are deemed important, but teachers see cognition as primary.
>
> American teacher–child relationships are focused on teacher authority and control. The aim is *compliance* (students conforming to an external standard) rather than *complicity* (internalization of the standard that results from identification with others).[8] While discipline is couched in a language of choice/self-control, it is ultimately not the child's choice or control over him- or herself, but the teacher's power over the child that results in compliance.[9]

In the second study,[10] a different American anthropologist followed a Japanese boy who, after preschool in Japan, spent over five years in the United

States. He then returned to Japan. His experience amplifies the differences between the meanings of "choice" in the two cultures.

In the United States, students had choices *during lessons*, such as with whom and where in the room they worked, but otherwise they were routinely monitored and constrained. In Japan, students had few choices during lessons (other than how they would contribute to the discussion), but a virtually unlimited range of options during their many breaks.

American teachers often used the word "choice" when reprimanding students regarding their behavior, as in, *If you choose to do X, then you'll be punished.* The anthropologist commented that "choosing implies freedom," but in the United States the teachers' message was that "there are good choices (following the rules) and bad choices (not following the rules)."

In Japan, talk of freedom to choose was rare. Teachers discussed behavior, but usually with the entire class, and when doing so framed the discussion around "how certain types of behavior were having a negative impact on human relations within the classroom."[11]

As you see, a case can be made that U.S. primary school classrooms are more teacher-centered (or -dominated) than those in East Asia.

Are U.S. or Chinese Classrooms More Student-Centered?

The following two studies share similarities. Completed by different Chinese researchers, both examined videotapes of seventh-grade mathematics lessons at schools in and near Shanghai.

In the first study,[12] a geometry teacher skillfully used procedural and conceptual variation, distributing "colored sticks" for the students to manually solidify their understanding. He posed questions, guided the students to explore, directed them to solve a problem in groups, and asked them to identify geometrical features. After each question or instruction, he waited for them to respond.

Was this teacher lecturing? No, he was guiding, facilitating, and scaffolding. He was not behaving like a quiz show host, either.

> The lesson unfolded smoothly, strictly following a deliberate design by the teacher. It would be labeled as a teacher-dominated lesson from a Western perspective. However, if students' involvement and contribution to the creation of these variations are taken into consideration, it is hard to say that students are passive learners.
>
> The characterization of Confucian-heritage classrooms as teacher-centered conceals important characteristics related to the agency accorded to the students, albeit an agency mediated by the teacher.[13]

The second study[14] concerned a seventh-grade lesson on equations. It began with a "situational question" (problem of the day) and ended with a "summary" in which students made observations and reached conclusions on their own. Two-thirds of class time was devoted to whole-class interaction, with the teacher asking questions and the students responding. The researcher noted that, "The students were consistently attentive and followed the teacher's instruction. There were no instances of either inattentiveness or off-task behavior."[15]

During post-lesson interviews, the teacher explained that *he drew on his understanding of how his students think to develop a "framed exploratory experience" for them.* He emphasized that, "I let the students investigate," "I let them try," and "I give them questions to think about."[16] About the lesson's summary, he said

> I asked such questions so that the students could discuss it and reach a conclusion. After the students had their discussion, we exchanged ideas. If the students' summary was not comprehensive enough, I would give some hints and we would then work out the conclusion together.[17]

Here are the researcher's own conclusions:

> All events closely followed this teacher's careful planning and expectations. One may conclude that the teacher was "dominating."
>
> But from the teacher's perspective, his lesson was definitely not teacher-dominated. *Each part of his lesson was supported by a student-oriented rationale,* which emphasized objectives such as helping students develop a capability, letting them try out their skills, and providing a foundation for further work. He gave serious consideration to the students' abilities, thinking, and participation. *In this sense, the teacher's design of the lesson is "student-centered."*[18]

So it's possible to make a case that East Asian primary school lessons are more student-centered than those in the United States.

One thing is clear: *The meanings of the terms "student-centered" and "teacher-centered" are shaped by the cultures in which they're being used.*

THE "CENTEREDNESS" OF CLASSROOMS VERSUS LESSONS

It's quite revealing that American educators and parents put so much emotional intensity into the issue of whether a classroom is "centered" on the teacher or the students. Absent Western influences, most people in East Asia don't worry about this issue. It's *our* concern.

Why do *we* care so much about this "centered" business?

It's a predictable feature of a culture that's become more and more individualistic since the latter decades of the nineteenth century. Youngsters learn to enact the behavior and values of individualism first by being with family members, then by attending the early grades in school, and later by other means. We *consciously care* that each child develops self-acceptance, self-confidence, self-expressiveness, self-reliance, self-assertiveness, creativity, and proud appreciation of his or her own unique qualities and abilities. We believe that a classroom that's consistently centered on the teacher simply won't do.

Sure, parents agree that adults should wield ultimate authority within schools. But those adults had better not run classrooms in ways that undermine attention to individual children's unique characteristics, special needs, preferred learning styles, and emerging creativity.

Many Americans agree that *gaining knowledge* is an important reason why children attend school. The knowledge they expect children to learn includes reading, writing, mathematics, and a variety of academic and other subjects, all of which are delivered to children via "lessons."

So let's shift from talking broadly about primary school classrooms, and instead narrow our attention to the characteristics of the lessons being taught there.

The three indispensable components of a lesson are the teacher, the students, and the knowledge to be learned. Let's ponder the implications of each as being where a lesson is "centered."

Implications of a Teacher-Centered Lesson

My belief always has been that, if a lesson is unmistakably teacher-centered, what's going on in the room is more about the teacher's self-aggrandizement than about anything related to the students.

My assumption about a teacher-centered (or -dominated) lesson is that he or she would behave in an emotionally distant, controlling manner, and would show little sustained interest in pupils' learning the material (individually or as a group), nor in their possible contributions to the lesson. Similarly, there would be little sustained interest in the children's quality of relationships with one another, in their overall social development, in their families' situations, or in their personal interests, needs, ideas, creative potential, and so forth.

I'm now recalling my high school teacher of geometry and calculus, Ms. Betty Bates, who some would say was delivering teacher-centered lessons. Others would say she was "old-school." I would say that she cared deeply about our learning geometry and calculus, and learning it well. In my memory of school days, she reigns as the best classroom teacher I ever had. She does not fit the narrow definition of teacher-centered that I'm using here.

My view is that teacher-centeredness of the self-aggrandizing variety is a perversion of the meaning, purpose, and promise of education. Fortunately, I'm convinced that that variety of teacher-centeredness is rare in both the United States and East Asia.

Implications of a Student-Centered Lesson

If a lesson is unmistakably student-centered, what's going on in the room is primarily about matters such as the students' needs, interests, ideas, creativity, learning capacities, and challenges in understanding the material, insofar as these are known by the teacher.

Maximum student-centeredness occurs when students are basically allowed to undertake whatever projects they wish. Because this path is taken by only a handful of private schools,[19] we won't dwell on it.

If a lesson were centered on the students, the teacher's choices—which topics to emphasize, what methods and materials to use, how to motivate the students to learn, how to actively engage them, where to focus time and attention during the lesson, and to what extent to respond to individual students' needs, questions, and ideas—would all be guided largely by the teacher's beliefs about what's the best outcome for the individual students.

This is where things become complicated. Assumptions about what's the best outcome for students vary widely. "Best outcome" could be about their well-being now, when they apply for college or specialized high school, or after they are adults. Teachers at a school with religious sponsorship might make student-centered choices that contrast sharply with those made by teachers at a progressive school or a school in an authoritarian society. Dozens of factors could easily become involved.

There's also the factor of *national culture*, which has been the focus of this book. As noted in earlier chapters, a key distinction between educators in the United States and East Asia is that we think of students as separate and distinct individuals, while they think of students as groups of similar individuals. Their view is epitomized by the Japanese educator quoted at the beginning of chapter 3: "The goal of education is the reduction of individual differences among children."[20] That guy wouldn't last a week in an American school!

Where our meaning of "student-centered" comes from: I can't think of "student-centered" in the American context without being reminded of Herbert Spencer, the late nineteenth century philosopher. More than any other individual, Spencer[21] is responsible for Americans' beliefs about how children learn best, thanks to his popular public lectures and his massively influential little book entitled *Education*. Referring to what children learn in school as a "plan of culture," Spencer offers seven guiding principles for ensuring that children learn. Here's his seventh:

> As a final test by which to judge any plan of culture comes this question: *Does it create a pleasurable excitement in the pupils?* When in doubt whether a particular mode or arrangement is or is not in harmony with the foregoing principles than some other, we may safely abide by this criterion.[22]

A few pages earlier in *Education*, Spencer had warmly approved of "efforts to make early education amusing" and added that "daily we more and more conform our plans to juvenile opinion."[23]

My view of "student-centered" in the American context is that it comes from Spencer: Teachers and other educators are expected to give a high priority to attending to the needs, ideas, and capabilities of each student and to conducting learning experiences that students will find, often if not always, "amusing" and "pleasurably exciting."

Nowadays, we don't use that stilted nineteenth century language. Instead, we talk about students' visibly having "fun" and being "engaged."

Implications of a Knowledge-Centered Lesson

If a lesson is unmistakably knowledge-centered, then what's going on in the room is fundamentally driven by the goal of enabling the students to master the material being taught.

It's essential to keep one thing in mind about a knowledge-centered lesson: We're talking about what's going on *during the lesson*. That leaves open the possibility that a teacher, at other times in the classroom, and at other places in or even beyond the school, might demonstrate sustained concern and support for the students' well-being as a social group, as separate and distinct individuals, or even as something akin to family members.

Lessons, however, are devoted 100% to students' learning the material. Ms. Betty Bates's geometry and calculus lessons were devoted to my, and my classmates', learning the material.

Recall in chapter 5 the section entitled "Teacher's 'Senior' Roles: Their Opportunities." It's clear that teachers in East Asia devote vast volumes of thought, time, and effort into caring for the well-being and social development of their students. It's just that when a lesson is being taught is *not* the time to attend to those matters.

As noted in chapter 4 about teachers in East Asia,

> the internal logic of the content they are teaching is the principal driver of how they organize their lessons. They pay little or no attention to factors such as

each pupil's personality, interests, creativity, need to be motivated, antipathy to homework, or "learning style."

Given most Americans' definition of student-centered, if a teacher isn't paying attention to those latter factors, then the lesson falls short of excellence.

People in East Asia have a different definition. Chapter 5 discussed the habit of teachers there of thinking about their students *as a unified group*:

> An important goal for teachers is to present the lesson content so that all their pupils will be able to understand it. Yes, this means that the teacher might progress a little slower than the most able children *could* keep up with, and a little too fast for the least able ones to grasp without extra effort. But that's O.K., because the key objective is for all the children to progress together.

As a master of her subject, the teacher is well equipped to make these judgments and to patiently assist individuals who are struggling—but *not during lessons*.

LESSONS IN EAST ASIA: KNOWLEDGE-CENTERED

The methods used to deliver lessons to pupils in East Asia often are branded as teacher-centered. This book should have convinced you that, with respect to lessons in the primary grades, such a claim is false. A far more accurate generalization is that the lessons are *directively facilitated* or *directively coordinated* by the teacher in such a way that the pupils as a whole class—and not just those who raise their hands—are frequently contributing in substantive, on-topic ways.

East Asian lessons are also often claimed to be *not* student-centered. If we use our American meaning of student-centered, that claim seems to have merit. But as we've seen, there's an alternative definition of what student-centered means—one that focuses on the whole class, draws on the teacher's awareness of how its members tend to think, and envisions delivering content in ways that require broad participation and advance all pupils' abilities.

But neither term accurately fits East Asian lessons. We've been trying to apply on the other side of the world two terms that originated here and gained our emotion-laden meanings. This recalls the old adage about pushing square pegs into round holes. It doesn't work.

My years of study of the voluminous research findings have brought me to the conclusion that the most accurate generalization about East Asian lessons is that they are knowledge-centered.

I've come to the conclusion that they're knowledge-centered because, to an extent rarely seen here in the United States, East Asian pupils and their teacher are united in their attention to the knowledge to be learned, with the pupils' attention to the knowledge being actively steered by the teacher.

Evidence for Knowledge-Centered Lessons in East Asia

Following are twelve compelling pieces of evidence for my conclusion that lessons in East Asian primary schools are knowledge-centered:

1. **Early pupil training:** In preschool and first grade, pupils are trained how to contribute to a lesson's efficient delivery: how to sit, focus their attention, ask to speak, respond when called on, and especially how to rearrange the room quickly to suit any teacher's intention. The result is a sharp increase in second grade and through high school of the time available during any lesson for on-task learning.

    Result: Children gain the ability to directly support the teacher's intentions as each lesson progresses. They share responsibility with their teachers for the efficient and effective progress of their lessons.

2. **Teachers' subject mastery:** As has often been confirmed, almost all teachers in East Asia are content experts in their academic specialties.

    Result: Teachers' thorough grasp of their academic specialties enables them to plan and present lessons that are genuinely knowledge-centered. Their frequent scaffolding, carefully planned to mitigate pupils' struggles to learn, helps to make whole-class interactive teaching a success. And at times when no lesson is in progress, the individual assistance they give to perplexed pupils is buttressed by their own full comprehension.

3. **Focus on The Basics:** It is expected that the indispensable first step in learning any skill or knowledge domain is mastery of The Basics, that is, the elements that provide the foundation for more practical and imaginative topics to follow. Doing this is understood by all to necessitate the use of imitation and repetition.

    Result: Once The Basics have been *mastered*—which means not only understood but infused into long-term memory—children are effortlessly able to call up that basic information to support their efficient acquisition of more complex, advanced, and creative knowledge.

4. **Knowledge-focused textbooks:** East Asian textbooks directly focus on the knowledge to be learned—straight up, no frills. Publishers make little or no attempt to cloak the knowledge in features that many Westerners believe will make it attractive and engaging to children.

Result: By laying out the knowledge step by step, not enfolding and obscuring it with stories and self-help devices that editors *think* will make it interesting and relevant, East Asian textbooks unambiguously specify which knowledge pupils are supposed to be gaining. A side benefit is that the textbooks are thin, lightweight, and inexpensive.

5. **Content-centered lesson design:** Teachers design lessons based on the internal logic of the content they are teaching. They pay little or no attention to external factors such as individual pupils' personalities, interests, creativity, need to be motivated, learning styles, and so forth. But they diligently do take into account how best to present the content so that *all* pupils in their class will benefit from the lesson.

   Result: The theme and focus of each lesson is the knowledge to be learned, its connection with recent learning, and exploration of various pathways to grasp and master it. The personal concerns of individual pupils virtually never are allowed to detract from this focus.

6. **Teachers' lesson planning:** As individuals and colleagues, teachers devote prodigious quantities of time and effort to the planning of each lesson. And teachers in small groups further devote countless hours to planning, discussing, and observing pilot lessons—the Lesson Study process—to improve the degree to which critically important lessons will be well understood by pupils. (Teachers' planning is supported by system-wide policies that ensure that they have substantial preparation time built into their daily schedules.)

   Result: How to most effectively present challenging knowledge to pupils of various ages is perennially a matter of individual and collegial concern for teachers in East Asia. In some cases their choices are the result of collegial planning, piloting, and data-driven decision-making.

7. **Coach/Athlete-type relationships:** Teachers' relationships with pupils resemble those of coaches and athletes in that teachers straightforwardly direct and counsel pupils in ways to improve their academic performance. (Most parents in East Asia relate to their children in similar ways.[24])

   Result: Teachers' investment in individual pupils' academic success is demonstrated, and the pupils benefit from their frequent professional advice.

8. **Inviolable lesson time:** When in session, lessons are wholly devoted to the teacher's directive facilitating (i.e., scaffolding) the pupils' content learning. It is not to be interrupted by pupils who didn't "get" something, nor by school-wide announcements. Individual pupils are not pulled out of lessons to participate in any other activity, not even in special tutoring.

Result: That knowledge acquisition is the school's highest priority is made clear multiple times every day. Pupils benefit from receiving, without interruption, their teachers' well-planned lessons from start to finish.

9. **Whole-class *interactive* learning:** This often-used teaching mode is both genuinely interactive and directively facilitated by the teacher. It is characterized by repeated teacher-pupil and pupil-pupil exchanges that are focused on the knowledge to be learned. Teachers call on pupils without regard to their volunteering. Pupils often are asked to critique the contributions of classmates who spoke before them.

   Result: Pupils participate actively in knowledge-focused discussions, both publicly with the teacher as well as within their small groups. Few off-topic comments can be heard when lessons are in progress. It's really quite difficult for pupils in East Asia to remain passive!

10. **Thoughtful questioning and answering:** Teachers ask numerous questions, the majority being open-ended (including *how* and *why* questions). They also ask pupils to explain to the class (a) the concepts and procedures being learned and (b) their own reasoning about the matter under discussion. Teachers will sometimes linger over a nuanced issue for multiple minutes in what has been termed "sticky probing." And during math lessons, different pupils often are asked to present their unique solutions to a problem.

    Result: Pupils are actively drawn into ever more comprehensive familiarity with the finer points of the knowledge to be learned.

11. **Attention to incorrect answers:** During math and other academic lessons, incorrect answers and faulty reasoning are routinely dissected during discussions. Rather than assuming the role of Sole Arbiter of Right and Wrong, teachers characteristically call on pupils to analyze and correct their classmates' errors of fact, reasoning, or calculation. This doesn't become adversarial; the spirit is "we're all tackling this problem together."

    Result: Specific attention to how erroneous conclusions were reached strengthens pupils' conceptual grasp of the content's intricacies.

12. **Characteristics of East Asian math classes:** Typical of math classes in primary schools are (a) beginning with a challenging "problem of the day"; (b) moving beyond calculations to emphasize the abstract/symbolic features of problems; (c) using a variety of conceptual and procedural approaches, including manipulatives, for fully explaining new material; (d) emphasizing connections (conceptual links) among mathematical ideas, facts, procedures, and basic regularities; and (e) expecting pupils to apply deductive reasoning and produce accurately stated formal proofs.

Result: Pupils make progress toward mastery of high-level mathematical thinking skills, which research has consistently found to be characteristic of students in East Asian countries.

A MIRROR FOR AMERICANS

As we look into the mirror of East Asian schooling, what do we notice about *our* schools and the values *we* apply when thinking about them?

- **Knowledge-centered lessons:** The mirror of East Asian schooling alerts us to the fact that the terms "knowledge-centered *lesson*" and "knowledge-centered *classroom*" mean different things.

  This is not a trivial distinction. It's a distinction that gets to the heart of why the students of East Asia gain an apparently unbeatable academic edge over all but a handful of their peers in the United States.

  "Knowledge-centered lesson" refers narrowly to what's going on while a lesson is in progress. "Knowledge-centered classroom" refers broadly to the overall culture of the classroom, day after day.

  Lessons in East Asia are persistently knowledge-centered. Classrooms in East Asia are not.

  How shall we characterize East Asian primary school *classrooms*? Over decades, researchers have reported that teachers strive to develop a warm and supportive relationship with each child, one that encompasses the whole child, that is, that is not skewed toward cognitive growth. Teachers devote an abundance of time and energy to a variety of supportive activities for their pupils' all-around development as human beings who identify with their groups and feel responsible for their well-being.

  But when a lesson begins, all that is set aside. Its objectives, its plan, its methods, and its delivery are marshaled by the teacher in a variety of ways that persistently involve *all* of the pupils in mentally grappling with the knowledge to be learned. Above are listed twelve of the ways in which teachers in East Asia have been able to do that.

  In my view, the knowledge-centered character of primary school lessons in East Asia is the single most important factor that gives children there a competitive academic edge and helps to account for their superior performance on the international comparative tests.

Over nearly half a century, children across East Asia have consistently demonstrated a grasp of academic knowledge superior to that of American children. What's different over there? Years of study brought me to realize that certain fundamental values shared among East Asians orient their educational practices in ways that differ substantially from ours.

This book and *The Drive to Learn* have been written in hopes that they will inspire us to become aware of the side effects of the relentlessly individualistic values that shape the ways in which we raise our children at home and educate them in our schools. Yes, it's inconceivable that we would ever abandon our vaunted individualism in favor of East Asian-style group orientation. Nonetheless, their ways of applying their values to education are useful as a mirror, for they help us to see ourselves as others see us. Informed by the contrasts that the East Asian mirror reveals, we can gain a less culture-bound perspective on our ways of raising and educating our youngest children, imagine possibilities, and begin to think creatively about improvements that will remain compatible with our individualistic ways of life.

My years of study leave me with this:

If improving the academic performance of American children ever becomes extremely important to us, then

1. Parents will find new ways to instill in their children *a drive to learn* that emphasizes receptiveness to learning in classroom settings; and
2. Teachers at the primary level will find new ways to plan and present *knowledge-centered lessons* that constantly and interactively immerse all of their pupils in reasoning and analysis about the knowledge to be learned, directively facilitated by the teacher.

FURTHER READING

If you'd like more detail about the researchers' findings, or simply wish to know what inspired the contents of chapter 9, read these entries in the annotated bibliography at www.amirrorforamericans.info.

- Huang, Rongjin, & Frederick K.S. Leung (2005), Deconstructing teacher-centeredness and student-centeredness dichotomy: A case study.
- Hoffman, Diane (2000), Individualism and individuality in American and Japanese early education.
- Damrow, Amy (2014), Navigating the structures of elementary school in the United States and Japan: An ethnography.
- Mok, Ida Ah Chee (2006), Shedding light on the East Asian learner paradox: Reconstructing student-centeredness in a Shanghai classroom.

Just published as *A Mirror for Americans* goes to press is a new book by the French cognitive psychologist Stanislas Dehaene: *How We Learn: Why Brains Learn Better Than Any Machine...For Now.*

Dehaene's book is largely devoted to helping readers grasp the awesome capacities of the human brain to learn an infinite variety of complex skills. When he considers formal schooling, he notes that for classroom learning to be effective, four "pillars of learning" are required: focused attention, active engagement, error feedback, and daily rehearsal and consolidation.

As *A Mirror for Americans* has explained, East Asian primary schools are good examples of Dehaene's four pillars being applied in day-to-day practice.

Postscript

The most important factor in determining whether readers can understand a text is how much relevant vocabulary or background knowledge they have . . . That, at least, is what scientists have concluded. Educators and professors of education, on the other hand, have come to exactly the opposite conclusions.

Journalist Natalie Wexler in
The Knowledge Gap[1]

Having devoted a decade to studying the findings of researchers who had explored why East Asian students learn better than their American peers, I had neglected to investigate the flip side of that question: Why do American students learn poorly?

Soon after submitting my manuscript to Rowman & Littlefield, I found that an American journalist had recently used anthropological methods to explore that very question. So I went right out and purchased Natalie Wexler's 2019 book, *The Knowledge Gap: The Hidden Cause of America's Broken Education System – And How to Fix It*. It was money well spent.

What do I mean by noting that Wexler "had recently used anthropological methods"? That means that she carried out her research, in part, in a manner similar to anthropologists, most notably by sitting in lower primary school classrooms hour after hour, observing and taking notes. The schools where she observed were in the District of Columbia, Reno, Baltimore, and Boston. She also delved into research, drew on prior analyses, and talked extensively with a wide range of individuals – not only with children, teachers, and administrators, but also with scientists such as Daniel Willingham and academics such as E.D. Hirsch.

A SUMMARY OF WHAT *THE KNOWLEDGE GAP* REVEALS

What grabbed my attention about Wexler's book was that *she and I had come to a virtually identical conclusion after following different pathways of inquiry*. I relied on research carried out in the classrooms of East Asia over the past thirty years, which led me to recognize that the advantage in East Asian lower-grade lessons is that attention to knowledge is paramount. Wexler relied on her own recent observations as well as the research and writings of others in the United States, which brought her to the conclusion that the deficiency in *our* lower-grade lessons is that attention to knowledge is *not* paramount.

As Wexler tells it, one day a veteran U.S. educator specializing in writing mentioned to her that "most elementary schools aren't even trying to teach anything of substance." To which Wexler responded, "What do you mean? They're *schools*, aren't they?" Not long after, she overheard someone else in the education field comment that someone should write a book about "this whole curriculum thing."[2] Wexler's curiosity was piqued. She decided to write that book.

Wexler undertook her project primarily to figure out why a majority of American students lack proficiency in reading.[3] Her quest yielded the answer. It's about the reigning belief of most American educators about how best to teach reading: In lower primary school, reading should be taught as a set of skills and strategies. What ought *not* to be taught are facts about the world (history, science, etc.), which are developmentally inappropriate. But after youngsters learn *how* to read, they'll become able to "construct" such factual knowledge for themselves.

LEARNING TO READ AND THE "READING WARS"

It's widely agreed that there are two components to learning how to read. What's led to the "Reading Wars" is the question of how best to teach each of those components.

The first is *decoding*, which is indispensable because what we read actually are squiggled lines on a surface. The learner must learn how to "decode" each squiggle into a sound, combine isolated sounds into words, and so forth. The decoding controversy has been between the proponents of "phonics," which calls for systematic and explicit teaching of decoding skills, versus "whole language," which argues that "children will naturally pick up the ability to read and write if allowed to choose books and topics that interest them."[4] Scientists have come down solidly in favor of phonics.

Wexler became more interested in the other indispensable component of reading: *comprehension*. After fledgling readers learn to decode squiggles into sounds, and sounds into words, they must become able to recognize the meaning of each separate word, and of all the words together. The teaching of comprehension has also been the focus of controversy. That's the principal focus of *The Knowledge Gap*.

On one side are those who argue that new readers should be taught the skills and strategies employed by advanced readers, so that—or so their argument goes—they'll learn how to comprehend just about anything they read. Examples of skills are "find the main idea," "identify the supporting details," and the like; examples of strategies are "ask yourself questions about the text," "pause periodically to summarize," and the like.[5] Those on this side of the controversy are claiming that these skills, once mastered, can be used to understand any text.

On the other side are those who argue that such skills and strategies are of little use to anyone who knows nothing about the topic of a text. Why? Because authors inevitably leave basic information out of their texts; they expect readers to be able to supply it. But if readers don't have the background knowledge to do that, they're out of luck! What fledgling readers need is a growing knowledge of the world *and* a vocabulary that grows along with it.

That necessity, knowledge of the world, accounts for the title of Wexler's book. It's her contention that American students are repeatedly shown to read poorly because the subjects that can build knowledge of the world—history, science, geography, art, literature, and more—are rarely taught in the early grades, leaving a gap that undermines their ability to comprehend texts.

So why have those subjects been overlooked? *They haven't been!* We're talking about a wide-eyed, deliberate choice made by the U.S. education establishment, which believes that young pupils can't handle abstract knowledge and will become frustrated and discouraged if they try. There's no scientific evidence to support the establishment's belief.

WHAT DOES SCIENCE SAY ABOUT COMPREHENSION?

The principal value from *The Knowledge Gap* comes from Wexler's marshalling of the science supporting the view that to learn rapidly and well, beginning readers need a growing vocabulary and, especially, a growing knowledge of the world. (Obviously, these two factors are related.)

But I'm not going to review the scientific consensus here. I'm going to urge you to devote ten minutes to watch a YouTube video made by psychologist

Daniel Willingham.[6] Early in his career, Willingham decided "to do whatever he could to communicate the findings of cognitive science directly to practicing teachers."[7] I learned about this video from reading Wexler's book. I now commend it to you. Entitled "Teaching Content *Is* Teaching Reading," this video is *not* of the talking-head variety. (Willingham's head is visible for only a few seconds.) I found his innovative presentation not only straightforward and clear but also amusing.

Learning to read requires youngsters (a) to learn how to decode and then (b) to increasingly become able to grasp the meaning of whatever they're reading *because of the knowledge of the world they bring to it.* Readers with little worldly knowledge will be severely handicapped by passages about things and ideas beyond their own narrow experience; no amount of skill or strategy can compensate for an absence of foundational knowledge. So to paraphrase Willingham, teaching anything of substance *is* the teaching of reading.

Regarding unequal learning outcomes for students from different backgrounds, Wexler points to "the Matthew effect."[8] In the Gospel of Matthew there's a verse[9] that states, "For unto every one that hath shall be given, and he shall have abundance; but from him that hath not, even that which he hath shall be taken away." Simply put: the rich get richer and the poor get poorer. Simply put *educationally*: children who've learned a great deal about the wider world from their families arrive at school with a huge head start in learning to read. By teaching very little "content" in the early grades, educators do nothing to level the playing field. So those who start out with more knowledge will continue to accumulate more and more every year, while their less fortunate age-peers will fall ever farther behind

Early in *The Knowledge Gap*, Wexler offers her "bottom line" on why American students are woefully deficient in reading: "The test-score gap is, at its heart, a knowledge gap."[10]

A Mirror for Americans doesn't focus on reading, but my bottom line is virtually identical to Wexler's. I'll state it as a question: "Our educators have decided that our youngest students will be taught very little knowledge, so why are they always surprised when they score poorly on tests that depend on children's accumulated knowledge?"

The underlying question is: "Why do so many Americans give so little respect to science?"

Bibliography

[A] = the cited item is included in the online annotated bibliography

An, Shuhua, Gerald Kulm, & Zonghe Wu (2004). The pedagogical content knowledge of middle school mathematics teachers in China and the U.S. *Journal of Mathematics Teacher Education, 7* (2), 145–172.

"April" (2017). Lesson studies in China. lessonstudychina.wordpress.com/lesson-studies-in-china/.

Becker, Jerry P., Toshio Sawada, & Yoshinori Shimizu (1999). Some findings of the US–Japan cross-cultural research on students' problem-solving behaviors. *International Comparisons in Mathematics Education*, Gabriele Kaiser et al., eds. Falmer Press, 121–139. [A]

Behaene, Stanislas (2020). *How We Learn: Why Brains Learn Better Than Any Machine...for Now.* Penguin, 305 pages.

Ben-Ari, Eyal (1997). *Body Projects in Japanese Childcare: Culture, Organization, and Emotions in Preschool.* Routledge, 165 pages. [A]

Bernstein, Marc F. (2016, August 24). Who should be responsible for student learning? Commentary section, *Education Week, 28,* 32.

Biggs, John B. (1996). Western misperceptions of the Confucian heritage learning culture. *The Chinese Learner: Cultural, Psychological, and Contextual Influences,* D. A. Watkins & J. B. Biggs, eds. Comparative Education Research Centre [Hong Kong] and Australian Council for Educational Research, 45–68.

Biggs, John B. (2001). Teaching across cultures. *Student Motivation: The Culture and Context of Learning,* Farideh Salili et al., eds. Kluwer Academic/Plenum, 293–308. [A]

Bjork, Christopher (2016). *High-Stakes Schooling: What We Can Learn from Japan's Experiences with Testing, Accountability, and Education Reform.* University of Chicago Press, 251 pages. [A]

Bjork, Christopher, & Ryoko Tsuneyoshi (2005). Education reform in Japan: Competing visions for the future. *Phi Delta Kappan, 86* (1), 619–626.

Brooks, David (2015). The moral bucket list. *The New York Times*, April 11, 2015. www.nytimes.com/2015/04/12/opinion/sunday/david-brooks-the-moral-bucket-lis t.html.

Brown, Lyn Mikel, & Jenny Flaumenhaft (2018). Student-powered curricular change. *Phi Delta Kappan, 100* (6), 13–19.

Burns, Robert (1786). To a louse, on seeing one on a lady's Bonnet at church. *Poetical Works of Robert Burns*, Logie Robertson, ed. (1896). Henry Frowde.

Cai, Jinfa (2005). U.S. and Chinese teachers' constructing, knowing, and evaluating representations to teach mathematics. *Mathematical Thinking and Learning, 7* (2), 135–169. [A]

Cai, Jinfa, & Victor Cifarelli (2004). Thinking mathematically by Chinese learners: A cross-national perspective. *How Chinese Learn Mathematics: Perspectives from Insiders*, Lianghuo Fan et al., eds. Series on Mathematics Education, Vol. 1. World Scientific, 71–106. [A]

Cai, Jinfa, & Tao Wang (2009). Conceptions of effective mathematics teaching within a cultural context: Perspectives of teachers from China and the United States. *Journal of Mathematics Teacher Education, 13* (3), 265–287. [A]

Cambridge University (2009). *News*. Cam.ac.uk/news/socrates-was-guilty-as-ch arged.

Chao, Ruth, & Vivian Tseng (2002). Parenting in Asia. *Handbook of Parenting*, 2nd Ed., Vol. 4. Marc Bornstein, ed. Erlbaum, 59–93.

Che, Yi, Akiko Hayashi, & Joseph Tobin (2007). Lessons from China and Japan for preschool practice in the United States. *Educational Perspectives, 40* (1), 7–12. [A]

Chen, Chuansheng, Shin-ying Lee, & Harold W. Stevenson (1996). Academic achievement and motivation of Chinese students: A cross-national perspective. *Growing Up the Chinese Way: Chinese Child and Adolescent Development*, Sing Lau, ed. The Chinese University Press, 69–91. [A]

Chen, Chuansheng, & David Uttal (1988). Cultural values, parents' beliefs, and children's achievement in the United States and China. *Human Development, 31*, 351–358.

Cheng, Kai-ming (1998). Can education values be borrowed? Looking into cultural differences. *Peabody Journal of Education, 73* (2), 11–30. [A]

Cheng, Rebecca Wing-yi, Tse-Mei Shu, Ning Zhou, & Shui-fong Lam (2016). Motivation of Chinese learners: An integration of etic and emic approaches. *The Psychology of Asian Learners: A Festschrift in Honor of David Watkins*, Ronnel B. King & Alan B. I. Bernardo, eds. Springer Singapore, 355–368. [A]

Chu, Lenora (2017). *Little Soldiers: An American Boy, a Chinese School, and the Global Race to Achieve*. HarperCollins, 347 pages. [A]

Clarke, David, & Li Hua Xu (2008). Distinguishing between mathematics classrooms in Australia, China, Japan, Korea, and the United States through the lens of the distribution of responsibility for knowledge generation: Public oral interactivity and mathematical orality. *ZDM, The International Journal of Mathematics Education, 40* (6), 963–972. [A]

Corden, Roy (2001). Group discussion and the importance of a shared perspective: Learning from collaborative research. *Qualitative Research, 1* (3), 347–367.

Cortazzi, Martin (1998). Learning from Asian lessons: Cultural expectations and classroom talk. *Education 3–13, 26* (2), 42–49. [A]

Cortazzi, Martin, & Lixian Jin (1996). Cultures of learning: Language classrooms in China. *Society and the Language Classroom*, Hywel Coleman, ed. Cambridge University Press, 169–206. [A]

Cortazzi, Martin, & Lixian Jin (2001). Large classes in China: 'Good' teachers and interaction. *Teaching the Chinese Learner: Psychological and Pedagogical Perspectives*, David A. Watkins & John B. Biggs, eds. Comparative Education Research Center, University of Hong Kong, 115–134. [A]

Cuban, Larry (1993). *How Teachers Taught: Constancy and Change in American Classrooms, 1890–1990*, 2nd Ed. Teachers College Press, 292 pages.

Dai, Qin, & Ka Luen Cheung (2015). The wisdom of traditional mathematical teaching in China. *How Chinese Learn Mathematics: Perspectives from Insiders* [2nd vol.], Lianghuo Fan et al., eds. Series on Mathematics Education, Vol. 6. World Scientific, 71–106. [A]

Damrow, Amy (2014). Navigating the structures of elementary school in the United States and Japan: An ethnography of the particular. *Anthropology & Education Quarterly, 45* (1), 87–104. [A]

Davin, Delia (1991). The early childhood education of the only child generation in urban China. *Chinese Education: Problems, Policies, and Prospects*, Irving Epstein, ed. Garland Publishing, 42–65. [A]

Della-Iacovo, Belinda (2009). Curriculum reform and 'Quality Education' in China: An overview. *International Journal of Educational Development, 29* (3), 241–249.

Dweck, Carol (2007). *Mindset: The New Psychology of Success*. Random House, 277 pages.

Fan, Lianghuo, & Yan Zhu (2007). Representation of problem-solving procedures: A comparative look at China, Singapore, and U.S. mathematics textbooks. *Educational Studies in Mathematics, 66*, 61–75. [A]

Fan, Lianghuo, Ngai-Ying Wong, Cai Jinfa, & Li Shiqi, eds. (2015). *How Chinese Teach Mathematics: Perspectives from Insiders*. Volume 6. World Scientific, 735 pages.

Fernandez, Clea, & Makoto Yoshida (2004). *Lesson Study: A Japanese Approach to Improving Mathematics Teaching and Learning*. Lawrence Erlbaum, 250 pages. [A]

Frkovich, Ann (2015). Taking it with you: Teacher education and the baggage of cultural dialogue. *Frontiers of Education in China, 10* (2), 175–200. [A]

Gao, Lingbiao (1998). Cultural context of school science teaching and learning in the People's Republic of China. *Science Education, 82* (1), 1–13. [A]

Gardner, Howard (1989). *To Open Minds: Chinese Clues to the Dilemma of Contemporary Education*. Basic Books, 325 pages (with photo illustrations). [A]

Geary, David C., C. Christine Bow-Thomas, Liu Fan, & Robert S. Siegler (1993). Even before formal instruction, Chinese children outperform American children in mental addition. *Cognitive Development, 8* (4), 517–529.

Greene, Jay P., & Josh B. McGee (2012). When the best is mediocre: Developed countries our most affluent suburbs [sic]. *Education Next, 12* (1), 34–40.

Grove, Cornelius (1977). *Cross-Cultural and Other Problems Affecting the Education of Immigrant Portuguese Students in a Program of Transitional Bilingual Education: A Descriptive Case Study*. Ed.D. dissertation, Teachers College, Columbia University. 403 pages. University Microfilms #77-14,722.

Grove, Cornelius (2006). Understanding the two instructional style prototypes: Pathways to success in internationally diverse classrooms. *Intercultural Communication Competencies in Higher Education and Management*, S.-H. Ong et al., eds. Marshall Cavendish Academic, 165–202.

Grove, Cornelius (2013). *The Aptitude Myth: How an Ancient Belief Came to Undermine Children's Learning Today*. Rowman & Littlefield, 187 pages.

Grove, Cornelius (2017a). Cognitive styles across cultures. *The International Encyclopedia of Intercultural Communication*, Young Yun Kim, ed. John Wiley & Sons.

Grove, Cornelius (2017b). Pedagogy across cultures. *The International Encyclopedia of Intercultural Communication*, Young Yun Kim, ed. John Wiley & Sons.

Grove, Cornelius (2017c). *The Drive to Learn: What the East Asian Experience Tells Us about Raising Students Who Excel*. Rowman & Littlefield, 153 pages.

Gu, Lingyuan, Rongjin Huang, & Ference Marton (2004). Teaching with variation: A Chinese way of promoting effective mathematics learning. *How Chinese Learn Mathematics: Perspectives from Insiders*, Lianghuo Fan et al., eds. Series on Mathematics Education, Vol. 1. World Scientific, 309–347. [A]

Hayashi, Akiko, Mayumi Karasawa, & Joseph Tobin (2009). The Japanese preschool's pedagogy of feeling: Cultural strategies for supporting young children's emotional development. *Ethos, 37* (1), 32–49. [A]

Hendry, Joy (1986). *Becoming Japanese: The World of the Pre-School Child*. University of Hawaii Press, 194 pages. [A]

Hess, Robert D., & Hiroshi Azuma (1991). Cultural support for schooling: Contrasts between Japan and the United States. *Educational Researcher, 20* (9), 2–8, 12. [A]

Hiebert, James, James Stigler, Jennifer Jacobs, Karen Givvin, Helen Garnier, Margaret Smith, Hilary Hollingsworth, Alfred Manaster, Diana Wearne, & Ronald Gallimore (2005). Mathematics teaching in the United States today (and tomorrow): Results from the TIMSS 1999 Video Study. *Educational Evaluation and Policy Analysis, 27* (2), 111–132. [A]

Ho, Irene T. (2001). Are Chinese teachers authoritarian? *Teaching the Chinese Learner: Psychological and Pedagogical Perspectives*, David A. Watkins & John B. Biggs, eds. Comparative Education Research Center, University of Hong Kong, 99–114. [A]

Hoffman, Diane M. (2000). Individualism and individuality in American and Japanese early education: A review and critique. *American Journal of Education, 108*, 300–317. [A]

Holloway, Susan D. (1988). Concepts of ability and effort in Japan and the United States. *Review of Educational Research, 58* (3), 327–345. [A]

Holloway, Susan D. (2000). *Contested Childhood: Diversity and Change in Japanese Preschools*. Routledge, 240 pages. [A]

Hu, Guangwei (2002). Potential cultural resistance to pedagogical imports: The case of communicative language teaching in China. *Language, Culture, and Curriculum, 15* (2), 93–105. [A]

Huang, Rongjin, & Frederick K. S. Leung (2005). Deconstructing teacher-centeredness and student-centeredness dichotomy: A case study of a Shanghai mathematics lesson. *The Mathematics Educator, 15* (2), 35–41. [A]

Hurd, Jacqueline, & Catherine Lewis (2011). *Lesson Study Step by Step: How Teacher Learning Communities Improve Instruction.* Heinemann, 176 pages.

Jin, Lixian, & Martin Cortazzi (1998). Dimensions of dialogue: Large classes in China. *International Journal of Educational Research, 29* (8), 739–761. [A]

Jin, Lixian, & Martin Cortazzi (2006). Changing practices in Chinese cultures of learning. *Language, Culture, and Curriculum, 19* (1), 5–20. [A]

Kawanaka, Takako, James W. Stigler, & James Hiebert (1999). Studying mathematics classrooms in Germany, Japan, and the United States: Lessons from the TIMSS videotape study. *International Comparisons in Mathematics Education*, Gabriele Kaiser et al., eds. Falmer Press, 86–103. [A]

Kelly, Kevin (1994). *Out of Control: The New Biology of Machines, Social Systems and the Economic World.* Addison-Wesley, 528 pages.

Kember, David (2016). Understanding and teaching the Chinese learner: Resolving the paradox of the Chinese learner. *The Psychology of Asian Learners: A Festschrift in Honor of David Watkins*, Ronnel B. King & Alan B. I. Bernardo, eds. Springer Singapore, 173–187. [A]

Kim, Terri (2009). Confucianism, modernities, and knowledge: China, South Korea, and Japan. *International Handbook of Comparative Education*, R. Cowen & A. M. Kazamias, eds. Springer Science, 857–872. [A]

Kotloff, Lauren J. (1998). ". . . And Tomoko wrote this song for us." *Teaching and Learning in Japan*, Thomas P. Rohlen & Gerald K. LeTendre, eds. Cambridge University Press, 98–118. [A]

Kwok, Percy (2004). Examination-oriented knowledge and value transformation in East Asian cram schools. *Asia Pacific Education Review, 5* (1), 64–75.

Lan, Xuezhao, Claire C. Ponitz, Kevin F. Miller, Su Li, Kai Cortina, Michelle Perry, & Ge Fang (2009). Keeping their attention: Classroom practices associated with behavioral engagement in first grade mathematics classes in China and the United States. *Early Childhood Research Quarterly, 24*, 198–211. [A]

Lancy, David F. (2015). *The Anthropology of Childhood*, 2nd Ed. Cambridge, 533 pages.

Lee, Shin-ying (1998). Mathematics learning and teaching in the school context: Reflections from cross-cultural comparisons. *Global Prospects for Education: Development, Culture, and Schooling*, S. G. Paris & H. M. Wellman, eds. American Psychological Association, 45–77. [A]

Lee, Shin-ying, Theresa Graham, & Harold W. Stevenson (1998). Teachers and teaching: Elementary schools in Japan and the United States. *Teaching and Learning in Japan*, Thomas P. Rohlen & Gerald K. LeTendre, eds. Cambridge University Press, 157–189. [A]

Leung, Frederick K. S. (2001). In search of an East Asian identity in mathematics education. *Educational Studies in Mathematics, 47*, 35–51. [A]

Lewis, Catherine (1991). Nursery schools: The transition from home to school. *Transcending Stereotypes: Discovering Japanese Culture and Education*, Barbara Finkelstein et al., eds. Intercultural Press, 81–95. [A]

Lewis, Catherine C. (1995). *Educating Hearts and Minds: Reflections on Japanese Preschool*. Cambridge University Press, 249 pages. [A]

Lewis, Catherine, & Ineko Tsuchida (1998). A lesson is like a swiftly flowing river: How research lessons improve Japanese education. *American Educator 22* (4), 12–17 & 50–52. [A]

Lewis, Ramon, Shlomo Romi, Xing Qui, & Yaacov J. Katz (2005). Teachers' classroom discipline and student misbehavior in Australia, China, and Israel. *Teaching and Teacher Education, 21*, 729–741. [A]

Li, Hui, X. Christine Wang, & Jessie Ming Sin Wong (2011). Early childhood curriculum reform in China. *Chinese Education & Society, 44* (6), 5–23. [A]

Li, Jin (2003). The core of Confucian learning. *American Psychologist, 58* (2), 146–147. [A]

Li, Jin (2012). *Cultural Foundations of Learning: East and West*. Cambridge, 385 pages. [A]

Li, Yeping (2007). Curriculum and culture: An exploratory examination of mathematics curriculum materials in their system and cultural contexts. *The Mathematics Educator, 10* (1), 21–38. [A]

Lim, Chap Sam (2007). Characteristics of mathematics teaching in Shanghai, China: Through the lens of a Malaysian. *Mathematics Education Research Journal, 19* (1), 77–88. [A]

Lin, Delia (2010). The cultural dilemma of a knowledge society in China: The case of "Education for Quality." *Regional Outlook Paper No. 24*, Griffith Asia Institute.

Linn, Marcia, Catherine Lewis, Ineko Tsuchida, & Nancy B. Songer (2000). Beyond fourth-grade science: Why do U.S. and Japanese students diverge? *Educational Researcher, 29* (3), 4–14. [A]

Liu, Jeng (2012). Does cram schooling matter? Who goes to cram schools? Evidence from Taiwan. *International Journal of Educational Development, 32*, 46–52.

Ma, Liping (1999). *Knowing and Teaching Elementary Mathematics: Teachers' Understanding of Fundamental Mathematics in China and the United States*. Lawrence Erlbaum, 232 pages. As reviewed by Roger Howe (1999), *Notes of the American Mathematical Society, 46* (8), 881–887. [A]

Makihara, Kumiko (2018). *Dear Diary Boy: An Exacting Mother, Her Free-Spirited Son, and Their Bittersweet Adventures in an Elite Japanese School*. Arcade, 218 pages. [A]

Marton, Ference (2000). Some critical features of learning environments. Invited keynote address, The Bank of Sweden Tercentenary Symposium on Cognition, Education, and Communication Technology. Stockholm, March 30–April 1. [A]

Marton, Ference, Amy B. M. Tsui, Pakey P. M. Chik, Po Yuk Ko, & Mun Ling Lo (2004). *Classroom Discourse and the Space of Learning*. Routledge, 256 pages.

McCarthy, Dorothea (1930). *The Language Development of the Pre-school Child*. University of Minnesota Press.

Mead, Margaret (1928). *Coming of Age in Samoa: A Psychological Study of Primitive Youth for Western Civilization*. Perennial Classsics (2001).

Miller, Peggy J., Su-hua Wang, Todd Sandel, & Grace E. Cho (2002). Self-esteem as folk theory: A comparison of European American and Taiwanese mothers' beliefs. *Parenting: Science and Practice, 2* (3), 209–239.

Mok, Ida Ah Chee (2006). Shedding light on the East Asian learner paradox: Reconstructing student-centeredness in a Shanghai classroom. *Asia Pacific Journal of Education, 26* (2), 131–142. [A]

Mok, Ida A. C., & Paul Morris (2001). The metamorphosis of the 'virtuoso': Pedagogic patterns in Hong Kong primary mathematics classrooms. *Teaching and Teacher Education, 17* (4), 455–468. [A]

Monbushō [Ministry of Education, Science, and Culture] (1989). *Yōchien kyōiku yōryō* [Guidelines for preschool education]. Tokyo.

Ng, Sharon S. N., & Nirmala Rao (2008). Mathematics teaching during the early years in Hong Kong: A reflection of constructivism with Chinese characteristics? *Early Years, 28* (2), 159–172. [A]

Nystrand, Martin (1996). *Opening Dialogue: Understanding the Dynamics of Language and Learning in the English Classroom.* Teachers College Press, 160 pages.

Orlick, Terry, Qi-ying Zhou, & John Partington (1990). Cooperation and conflict within Chinese and Canadian kindergarten settings. *Canadian Journal of Behavioural Science, 22* (1), 20–25. [A]

Ouyang, Huhua (2003). Resistance to the communicative method of language instruction within a progressive Chinese University. *Local Meanings, Global Schooling: Anthropology and World Culture Theory*, Kathryn M. Anderson-Levitt, ed. Palgrave Macmillan, 122–140. [A]

Paine, Lynn Webster (1990). The teacher as virtuoso: A Chinese model for teaching. *Teachers College Record, 92* (1), 49–81. [A]

Park, Kyungmee, & Frederick K. S. Leung (2006). A comparative study of the mathematics textbooks of China, England, Japan, Korea, and the United States. *Mathematics Education in Different Cultural Traditions: A Comparative Study of East Asia and the West*, F. K. S. Leung et al., eds. Springer, 227–238. [A]

Pashler, Harold, Mark McDaniel, Doug Rohrer, & Robert Bjork (2009). Learning styles: Concepts and evidence. *Psychological Science in the Public Interest, 9* (3), 105–119.

Peak, Lois (1991a). *Learning to Go to School in Japan: The Transition from Home to Preschool Life.* University of California Press, 210 pages. [A]

Peak, Lois (1991b). Training learning skills and attitudes in Japanese early education settings. *Transcending Stereotypes: Discovering Japanese Culture and Education*, Barbara Finkelstein et al., eds. Intercultural Press, 96–108. [A]

Perry, Michelle (2000). Explanation of mathematical concepts in Japanese, Chinese, and U.S. first- and fifth-grade classrooms. *Cognition and Instruction, 18* (2), 181–207. [A]

Perry, Michelle, Scott W. VanderStoep, & Shirley L. Yu (1993). Asking questions in first-grade mathematics classes: Potential influences on mathematical thought. *Journal of Educational Psychology, 85* (1), 31–40. [A]

Pratt, Daniel D., Mavis Kelly, & Winnie Wong (1998). The social construction of Chinese models of teaching. Adult Education Research Conference (San Antonio,

TX), unpaginated. newprairiepress.org/cgi/viewcontent.cgi?referer=&httpsredir=&article= 2019&context=aerc. [A]

Pratt, Daniel D., Mavis Kelly, & Winnie S. S. Wong (1999). Chinese conceptions of "effective teaching" in Hong Kong: Towards culturally sensitive evaluation of teaching. *International Journal of Lifelong Education, 18* (4), 241–258. [A]

Rao, Nirmala, Sharon S. N. Ng, & Emma Pearson (2009). Preschool pedagogy: A fusion of traditional Chinese beliefs and contemporary notions of appropriate practice. *Revisiting the Chinese Learner: Changing Contexts, Changing Education*, Carol K. K. Chan & Nirmala Rao, eds. Comparative Education Research Centre, 255–279. [A]

Rao, Nirmala, Emma Pearson, Kai-ming Cheng, & Margaret Taplin (2013a). *Teaching in Primary Schools in China and India: Contexts of Learning*. Routledge, 202 pages. [A]

Rao, Nirmala, Emma Pearson, Kai-ming Cheng, & Margaret Taplin (2013b). The classroom context: Teaching and learning language. *Teaching in Primary Schools in China and India: Contexts of Learning*. Routledge, 80–97. [A]

Ravitch, Diane (2007). *EdSpeak: A Glossary of Education Terms, Phrases, Buzzwords, and Jargon*. ASCD, 245 pages.

Reznitskaya, Alina, Richard Anderson, & Li-Jen Kuo (2007). Teaching and learning argumentation. *Elementary School Journal, 107* (5), 449–472.

Ripley, Amanda (2013). *The Smartest Kids in the World: And How They Got that Way*. Simon & Schuster, 306 pages.

Rohlen, Thomas P. (1997). Differences that make a difference: Explaining Japan's success. *The Challenge of Eastern Asian Education*, William K. Cummings & Philip G. Altbach, eds. State University of New York Press, 223–248. [A]

Rohlen, Thomas P., & Gerald K. LeTendre (1998a). Introduction: Japanese theories of learning. *Teaching and Learning in Japan*, Thomas P. Rohlen & Gerald K. LeTendre, eds. Cambridge University Press, 1–15. [A]

Rohlen, Thomas P., & Gerald K. LeTendre (1998b). Conclusion: Themes in the Japanese culture of learning. *Teaching and Learning in Japan*, Thomas P. Rohlen & Gerald K. LeTendre, eds. Cambridge University Press, 369–376. [A]

Rother, Mike (n.d.). www-personal.umich.edu/~mrother/Kata_Creates_Culture.html (a page of his Toyota Kata Website).

Russell, Nancy Ukai (1997). Lessons from Japanese cram schools. *The Challenge of Eastern Asian Education*, William K. Cummings & Philip G. Altbach, eds. State University of New York Press, 153–172. [A]

Salili, Farideh (2001). Teacher–student interaction: Attributional implications and effectiveness of teachers' evaluative feedback. *Teaching the Chinese Learner: Psychological and Pedagogical Perspectives*, David A. Watkins & John B. Biggs, eds. Comparative Education Research Center, University of Hong Kong, 77–98. [A]

Salzman, Mark (1986). *Iron and Silk*. Random House, 211 pages.

Santrock, John W. (2004). A topical approach to life-span development. *Cognitive Development Approaches*. McGraw-Hill, 200–225.

Sato, Nancy E. (2004). *Inside Japanese Classrooms: The Heart of Education*. Taylor & Francis (Routledge), 325 pages. [A]

Sato, Nancy, & Milbrey W. McLaughlin (1992). Context matters: Teaching in Japan and the United States. *Phi Delta Kappan, 73* (1), 359–366. [A]

Schleppenbach, Meg, Michelle Perry, Kevin F. Miller, Linda Sims, & Ge Fang (2007). The answer is only the beginning: Extended discourse in Chinese and U.S. mathematics classrooms. *Journal of Educational Psychology, 99* (2), 380–396. [A]

Sekiguchi, Yasuhiro, & Mikio Miyazaki (2000). Argumentation and mathematical proof in Japan. *International Newsletter on the Teaching and Learning of Mathematical Proof*, January/February issue. 7 pages (unpaginated). [A]

Shimahara, Nobuo K., & Akira Sakai (1992). Teacher internship and the culture of teaching in Japan. *British Journal of Sociology of Education, 13* (2), 147–162.

Shimahara, Nobuo K., & Akira Sakai (1995). *Learning to Teach in Two Cultures: Japan and the United States.* Garland Publishing, 259 pages. [A]

Shortz, Will (2019). 10 years of KenKen in The Times. *The New York Times*, 9 February 2019, 2.

Shimizu, Yoshinori (1999). Aspects of mathematics teacher education in Japan: Focusing on teachers' roles. *Journal of Mathematics Teacher Education, 2*, 107–116. [A]

Singleton, John (1991). *Gambaru*: A Japanese cultural theory of learning. *Transcending Stereotypes: Discovering Japanese Culture and Education*, Barbara Finkelstein et al., eds. Intercultural Press, 119–125. [A]

Spencer, Herbert (1878). *Education: Intellectual, Moral, and Physical.* University Press of the Pacific (2002), 238 pages.

Stevenson, Harold W., & James W. Stigler (1992). *The Learning Gap: Why Our Schools Are Failing and What We Can Learn from Japanese and Chinese Education.* Simon & Schuster (Touchstone), 237 pages. [A]

Stevenson, Harold W., & Shin-ying Lee (1990). Contexts for achievement: A study of American, Chinese, and Japanese children. *Monographs of the Society for Research in Child Development, 55* (1–2), Serial No. 221. Wiley, 119 pages. [A]

Stevenson, Harold W., & Shin-ying Lee (1997). The East Asian version of whole-class teaching. *The Challenge of Eastern Asian Education*, William K. Cummings & Philip G. Altbach, eds. State University of New York Press, 33–49. [A]

Stevenson, Harold W., Shin-ying Lee, James Stigler, Seiro Kitamura, Susumu Kimura, & Tadahisa Kato (1986). Learning to read Japanese. *Child Development and Education in Japan.* W. H. Freeman, 217–219.

Stigler, James W., & Harold Stevenson (1991). How Asian teachers polish each lesson to perfection. *American Educator, 15* (1), 12–21, 43–47. [A]

Stigler, James, & James Hiebert (1997). Understanding and improving classroom mathematics instruction: An overview of the TIMSS video study. *Raising Australian Standards in Mathematics and Science: Insights from TIMSS (Conference Proceedings).* Australian Council for Educational Research, 52–65. [A]

Stigler, James W., & James Hiebert (1999). *The Teaching Gap: Best Ideas from the World's Teachers for Improving Education in the Classroom.* The Free Press, 210 pages. [A]

Stigler, James W., & James Hiebert (2004). Improving mathematics teaching. *Educational Leadership, 61* (5), 12–17. [A]

Stigler, James W., & Michelle Perry (1990). Mathematics learning in Japanese, Chinese, and American classrooms. *Cultural Psychology*, J. Stigler et al., eds. Cambridge University Press, 328–353.

Stigler, James W., Clea Fernandez, & Makoto Yoshida (1998). Cultures of mathematics instruction in Japanese and American classrooms. *Teaching and Learning in Japan*, Thomas P. Rohlen & Gerald K. LeTendre, eds. Cambridge University Press, 213–247. [A]

Stimpfl, Joseph, Fuming Zheng, & William Meredith (1997). A garden in the motherland: A study of a preschool in China. *Early Child Development and Care, 129* (1), 11–26. [A]

Sugishita, Morihiro, & Kazufumi Omura (2001). Learning Chinese characters may improve visual recall. *Perceptual and Motor Skills, 93* (3), 579–594.

Tan, Charlene (2016). *Educational Policy Borrowing in China: Looking West or Looking East*. Routledge, 202 pages.

Tang, Catherine (1996). Collaborative learning: The latent dimension in Chinese students' learning. *The Chinese Learner: Cultural, Psychological, and Contextual Influences*, D. Watkins & J. Biggs, eds. Comparative Education Research Center, 183–204.

Tang, Degen, & Doug Absalom (1998). Teaching across cultures: Considerations for Western EFL teachers in China. *Hong Kong Journal of Applied Linguistics, 3* (2), 117–132. [A]

Teddlie, Charles, & Shujie Liu (2008). Examining teacher effectiveness within differentially effective primary schools in the People's Republic of China. *School Effectiveness and School Improvement, 19* (4), 387–407. [A]

The Coop School (Brooklyn, NY), webpage for its elementary school. TheCoopSch ool.org/programs/elementary-school/.

Tobin, Joseph J., David Y. H. Wu, & Dana H. Davidson (1991). Forming groups. *Transcending Stereotypes: Discovering Japanese Culture and Education*, Barbara Finkelstein et al., eds. Intercultural Press, 109–118. [A]

Tobin, Joseph, Yeh Hsueh, & Mayumi Karasawa (2009a). Chapter 2: China. *Preschool in Three Cultures Revisited*. University of Chicago Press, 22–94. [A]

Tobin, Joseph, Yeh Hsueh, & Mayumi Karasawa (2009b). Chapter 3: Japan. *Preschool in Three Cultures Revisited*. University of Chicago Press, 95–156. [A]

Tobin, Joseph, Yeh Hsueh, & Mayumi Karasawa (2009c). Chapter 4: United States. *Preschool in Three Cultures Revisited*. University of Chicago Press, 157–223. [A]

Tobin, Joseph, Yeh Hsueh, & Mayumi Karasawa (2009d). Chapter 5: Looking across time and cultures. *Preschool in Three Cultures Revisited*. University of Chicago Press, 224–248.

Tsoi, Grace (2013). In Hong Kong, the tutor as celebrity. *The New York Times*, August 18, 2013. www.nytimes.com/2013/08/19/world/asia/In-Hong-Kong-the-Tutor-as-Celebrity.html.

Tsuchida, Ineko, & Catherine C. Lewis (1998). Responsibility and learning: Some preliminary hypotheses about Japanese elementary classrooms. *Teaching and Learning in Japan*, Thomas Rohlen & Gerald K. LeTendre, eds. Cambridge University Press, 191–212. [A]

Tsukada, Mamoru (1991). Student perspectives on *Juku, Yobikō*, and the examination system. *Transcending Stereotypes: Discovering Japanese Culture and Education*, Barbara Finkelstein et al., eds. Intercultural Press, 178–182. [A]

Tsuneyoshi, Ryoko (2001). *The Japanese Model of Schooling: Comparisons with the United States*. Routledge, 219 pages. [A]

Tweed, Roger B., & Darrin R. Lehman (2002). Learning considered within a cultural context: Confucian and Socratic approaches. *American Psychologist, 57* (2), 89–99. [A]

Usui, Hiroshi (1996). Differences in teacher classroom behaviors in the United States and Japan: A field note. *Research and Clinical Center for Child Development Annual Report, 18* (3); Faculty of Education, Hokkaido University, 63–85. [A]

Van Egmond, Marieke, Ulrich Kühnen, & Jin Li (2013). Mind and virtue: The meaning of learning, a matter of culture. *Learning, Culture, and Social Organization, 2* (3), 209–210.

Vygotsky, Lev S. (1978). Interaction between learning and development. *Mind in Society: The Development of Higher Psychological Processes*, M. Cole et al., eds. Harvard University Press, 79–91.

Wallace, Guy W. (2011). Why is the research on learning styles still being dismissed by some learning leaders and practitioners? *eLearn Magazine*. https://elearnmag.ac m.org/featured.cfm?aid=2070611.

Wang, Tao, & John Murphy (2004). An examination of coherence in a Chinese mathematics classroom. *How Chinese Learn Mathematics: Perspectives from Insiders*, Lianghuo Fan et al., eds. Series on Mathematics Education, Vol. 1. World Scientific, 107–123. [A]

Watkins, David (2000). Learning and teaching: A cross-cultural perspective. *School Leadership & Management, 20* (2), 161–173. [A]

Weber, Keith, Carolyn Maher, Arthur Powell, & Hollylynne Stohl Lee (2008). Learning opportunities from group discussions: Warrants become the objects of debate. *Educational Studies in Mathematics, 68* (3), 247–261.

Wexler, Natalie (2019). *The Knowledge Gap: The Hidden Cause of America's Broken Education System – and How to Fix It*. Avery (Penguin Random House), 324 pages.

White, Merry (1993). School in the life of the teen. *The Material Child: Coming of Age in Japan and America*. The Free Press, 71–101. [A]

White, Merry I., & Robert A. LeVine (1986). What is an *ii ko* (good child)? *Child Development and Education in Japan*, Harold Stevenson et al., eds. W. H. Freeman, 59–62. [A]

Willingham, Daniel T. (2018). You're not a "visual learner." *The New York Times*, October 7, 2018, Sunday Review, 6.

Winner, Ellen (1989). How can Chinese children draw so well? *Journal of Aesthetic Education, 23* (1), 65–84; includes photos of children's art. [A]

Wong, N. Y., & K. M. Wong (1997). The mathematics curriculum of ten regions. *Mathmedia 82*, 82–84 [in Chinese].

Woodward, John, & Yumiko Ono (2004). Mathematics and academic diversity in Japan. *Journal of Learning Disabilities, 37* (1), 74–82. [A]

Wray, Harry (1999). *Japanese and American Education: Attitudes and Practices.* Bergin & Garvey, 322 pages. [A]

Yang, Yudong, & Thomas Ricks (2012). Chinese lesson study: Developing classroom instruction through collaborations in school-based Teaching Research Group activities. *How Chinese Teach Mathematics and Improve Teaching*, Yiping Li & Rongjin Huang, eds. Routledge, 51–65.

Yong, Zhang, & Yu Yue (2007). Causes for burnout among secondary and elementary school teachers and preventive strategies. *Chinese Education & Society, 40* (5), 78–85.

Zhang, Dianzhou, Shiqi Li, & Ruifen Tang (2004). The "two basics": Mathematics teaching and learning in mainland China. *How Chinese Learn Mathematics: Perspectives from Insiders*, Lianghuo Fan et al., eds. Series on Mathematics Education, Vol. 1. World Scientific, 189–201. [A]

Zhu, Yan, & Lianghuo Fan (2006). Focus on the representation of problem types in intended curriculum: A comparison of selected mathematics textbooks from mainland China and the United States. *International Journal of Science and Mathematics Education, 4*, 609–626. [A]